"THE BUCK STOPS HERE"

said

PRESIDENT HARRY TRUMAN

by
David M. Noyes
with
Edward J. Flynn

ISBN: 0-7596-4380-6 (E-book)
ISBN: 0-7596-4381-4 (Paperback)
ISBN: 1-4033-0589-7 (Hardcover)

This book is printed on acid free paper.

FOR "THE BUCK STOPS HERE" INFORMATION
edjflynn@aristotle.net
Book Orders:
1-800-338-1496

1stBooks - rev. 10/24/02

Acknowledgements
by
Edward J. Flynn

My thanks to Jenny and young David Noyes and his family for the many years of encouragement and help in getting this important project underway. My own family of critics, Edward, Louise and Catherine helped with never ending support. Bob Ferrell provided excellent guidance with his superior knowledge of Mr. Truman and with his own publishing background. Other Truman scholars like Alonzo Hamby, and Dr. Francis Heller...helped as well, as did John Toland.

I cannot overlook the great work of David McCullough in bringing Harry Truman and his administrations to so many people with his great, prizewinning book on the former President. He led the way for many others in print as well as on radio and TV and all Truman scholars are indebted to him.

Researchers at the Reference Department of the Central Arkansas Library System contributed immensely and I am grateful. Jack Hackethorn of Columbia, Missouri and Charles Gussman of Kansas City, Missouri, former roommates, were most helpful as well as Bill McLaughlin of Claremont, California.

The Truman Library staff members were most helpful over these many years. Liz Safley, Dennis Bilger and Pauline Testerman always went beyond the call to help. Raymond Geselbracht was in there to lend his support and it is appreciated. All my best to them.

Without Sandra Fleming I could not have gotten off the ground. Finally, the historical expertise, knowledge of the Presidency and English, plus her constant prodding to keep me on track, was a real contribution to the work and for which I have to thank profusely, Nina Cash.

This book is the work of David Noyes and he speaks throughout. Editing and re-writing and research to maintain clarity has been done by Edward J. Flynn.

<u>Dedication</u>

To the American People:

> "I base it on something fundamental. That is a knowledge of the people. For people never knowingly vote against themselves. Once they are given to understand what it is they are to vote for or against, they will know what to do."

> "The people are a great deal smarter than some credit them with."

> "Once they are convinced that they can trust you, the outcome is assured."

President Harry Truman on why he kept insisting that he would win the 1948 Presidential race.

Table of Contents

Preface

by

David Noyes

President Truman and I had a unique relationship. Neither he nor I initiated it; it just happened. A series of fortuitous and random events propelled us toward each other. I, for one, shall never be able to account fully for it. I was drawn to him. He seemed comfortable with me, and it was one of those rare relationships in which one sensed from the start a mutual empathy.

In my visits with him, I rarely brought him good news. Instead, I chose to bring him the bad news that he needed to know. Generally speaking, those in his inner circle had been reluctant to do this. He said to me one day, "The bad news is what I want to hear, and the good news will take care of itself. They don't usually give me all the bad news that I ought to have. Some keep telling me that I'm the greatest, but I have an inner voice that keeps telling me I'm not."

He paid little attention to his popularity ratings. Criticism or abuse in the press rarely troubled him if he was sure he was doing the right thing. History had taught him that many important decisions are only understood in retrospect, and that no action, however beneficial, would ever be received with total approbation. There would always be some segment, some group, some special interest that would be displeased. He had a curious way of putting it. "There are so many people in government who always try to keep an ear to the ground, as they put it, but when they do that, all they hear is the grasshoppers."

When it came to wrong decisions, Truman said, "I have no difficulty in making another decision to undo it. There is no pride of authorship or oversensitivity about having been wrong." It's no wonder that he never had difficulty sleeping soundly.

Although Truman was a devout historical scholar, he was not encumbered by any slavish adherence to precedent. "History tells us where we have been, but it doesn't tell us where we are going," he once said.

It was Harry Truman who was the first to refute the custom of imposing a heavy burden of reparation by the victor on the vanquished. But, he went one important step further: he undertook to restore and rebuild the fallen enemies, Germany and Japan, and ushered them into an era of prosperity, dignity, democracy, and commitment to the ways of peace.

His Marshall Plan and Point Four were totally new concepts in the history of international relations. On the domestic scene, he presented to the Congress an urgent recommendation for the passage of a Civil Rights Bill so long denied to so many of our citizens. In that effort, he met disappointment at the hands of those in Congress who were captives of a tradition and who prevented its adoption by a filibuster. Having lost this battle for civil rights, Truman at once invoked his executive power and ordered the military to desegregate.

In his conduct of the Presidency, Truman had displayed a remarkable sense of the future. He said to me once, "Part of my biggest responsibility is to sense what is in the offing." Anything a President has to do now, he will find himself from six months to a year too late. A President must anticipate and not procrastinate, once he knows what he must do. Inevitably there will be some mistakes, but if we have time, we can undo them."

It was Winston Churchill who inscribed in one of his books this eloquent tribute to Truman: "To the man responsible for saving Free Europe." Today, we see West Germany, a pillar of economic strength and a bulwark to a peaceful Europe. In Japan, there is a flourishing democracy and an industrial bastion such as that country never dreamed of, and all because President Harry Truman had the vision which impelled him to restore Japan.

Having demonstrated the awesome destructive power of nuclear energy in order to bring the war to a quick resolution, Truman moved to put its use to peace-keeping purposes by placing its custody in the United Nations. One can only speculate what might have happened had Russia not aborted this unique opportunity for an enforced peace.

Truman was not without his share of human frailties. He was almost always able to keep them under control except in those instances when personal attacks were made against his immediate family (music critic Hume and columnist Drew Pearson), or as in the case of U.S.S.R. Foreign Minister Molotov, where commitments made at Yalta had been breached. And then, of course, there was his proclivity for extending his loyalty to many who had long forfeited their right to it.

For me, the following event provides some insight into Truman's unique concept of the Presidency.

Where Tom Dewey failed in his bid to dislodge the Trumans from the White House, a hoard of tiny creatures, nesting, burrowing in the woodwork, succeeded. They rendered the living quarters unsafe, and in 1948, the President was forced to take up resident in the historic Blair House across the street. The Blair posed no special problems for the President, except for the annoyance of being hustled across Pennsylvania Avenue by a phalanx of Secret Service men in going to and from his office in the East Wing of the White House.

When finally the White House had been restored, HST asked me to accompany him on a tour of inspection. As we went from room to room, floor to floor, the President treated me to an exciting lesson in American history with a running account of all the previous alterations and additions to the White House, together with some pithy asides about its former occupants.

It was dusk when we found ourselves on the roof, and we stood there silently absorbed in all that was around us—the vast assemblage of government installations and the symbols of our past and present. It was a transcendental experience for me, being there on top of the building which housed the central authority of the nation, and standing next to the man in whom that authority was vested.

The silence was suddenly brokenly. "David..." I was instantly alerted; the President usually addressed me as "Dave," and only as "David" when he wanted to stress a point. "David, I hope that no future occupant of this citadel of the American people will tend to regard himself as the landlord instead of the tenant that he truly is."

Woodrow Wilson, in one of his essays about the Presidency, made a very succinct comment about what happens to those who cross the threshold into the White House: "Some swell, and some grow." Truman well knew the grandeur and the power that went with the Presidency, and while he always protected and defended it—at times fiercely—he viewed the office in terms of its enormous responsibilities and duties, and not in his celebrity or in a sense of personal power. He always referred to the Presidency in the third person, and he was deeply aware that he was on a limited assignment—as he expressed it to me that night on the roof of the White House.

Cast of Characters

Dean Acheson, Secretary of State under Harry Truman

Joe Alsop—One of two brothers who were reporters in Washington

Stewart Alsop—Washington reporter, brother to Joe Alsop

Barney Balaban, Head of Paramount Pictures, New York

Habib Bourguiba—President of Tunisia

General Omar Bradley—Army General, World War II

James F. Byrnes, Secretary of State under Harry Truman

Arthur Capper—Former U.S. Senator from Kansas

Whittaker Chambers—former *Time Magazine* editor

Winston Churchill—Prime Minister of Great Britain, 1945

Joe Collins—Lt. General in the U. S. Army, 1945

Matthew J. Connelly—Appointments Secretary for Mr. Truman

Rose Conway—Personal secretary to Mr. Truman

James M. Cox—Ohio newspaper publisher who ran for President in 1928

Elmer Davis, Radio commentator

Charles DeGaulle—French General, later Prime Minister of France

Tom Dewey—Former Governor of New York and presidential candidate against Truman

Allen Dulles—Brother of John Foster Dulles and second head of CIA

John Foster Dulles—Foreign Affairs diplomat in several administrations

Levi Eshkol—Prime Minister of Israel, 1946

Abraham Feinberg—Truman supporter

Harold Fendler—Los Angeles attorney for Harry Truman

Ben Gradus—Producer, "Decision" TV series

Andrei Gromyko—Soviet Ambassador to the United States

Warren G. Harding—29th President of the United States

Dr. Hertzog—Prime Minister's office, Israel; 6th President of Israel

John Hildring—General in the Army, 1942

Bill Hillman—Co-author with David Noyes on Truman Memoirs

Alger Hiss—Discredited State Department official

Harry Hopkins, Deputy to Franklin D. Roosevelt

Colonel E. M. House, Deputy to President Woodrow Wilson

Lyndon Baynes Johnson (LBJ)—36th President of the United States (1963-1969)

Jiang Kai Shek—Prime Minister of China

Estes Kefauver, Senator from Tennessee and candidate for President

Albert D. Lasker— President Harding's campaign manager and former advertising executive; Partner of David Noyes.

Trgyve Lie—First Secretary General of the United States

General George Marshall—U. S. Army Chief of Staff and later Secretary of State under Harry Truman

Thurgood Marshall—Solicitor General of the United States

Joe McCarthy—U. S. Senator (Republican) from Wisconsin

William McChesney Martin—Federal Reserve head under Mr. Truman

Merle Miller—TV Writer

Charles Murphy—White House Counsel under Mr. Truman

Gamal Abdul Nasser—President of Egypt (1956-70)

Donald Nelson—Head of the U. S. War Production Board, 1943-1946

Paul Nitze—Secretary of Navy, 1940

Richard Nixon—37th President of the United States

Lord Chief Justice Reading of Great Britain—British official who was asked to help in dealing with problems between Britain and the United States.

General Mathew Ridgeway—Former Army Chief of Staff

Mrs. Eleanor Roosevelt—Wife of 32nd U.S. President Franklin D. Roosevelt

Franklin D. Roosevelt—32nd President of the United States, 1936-1945

Elmo Roper—Polling executive.

Robert Sarnoff—Chairman of the Board of NBC, 1962

Burt Schneider—Motion picture producer, Columbia Pictures

Robert Seidelman—Sales Department head for Screen Gems

John Snyder—Secretary of the Treasury under Mr. Truman

Admiral Sidney Souers—First head of CIA

Adlai Stevenson—Former Governor of Illinois and candidate for President twice-failed each time

Henry L. Stimson-Secretary of War, 1939-1944

David Susskind—New York TV Producer

Kaptaro Suzuki-Japanese Prime Minister, 1945

Shigemoro Togo—Japanese Foreign Minister 1941-42

General Hoyt Vandenberg—Former Air Force General and second head of the CIA

General Van Fleet—U. S. Army General, World War II

Chief Justice Fred M. Vinson—Chief Justice of the Supreme Court in 1945

Henry Wallace—Secretary of Agriculture under Franklin Roosevelt who later ran for president against Mr. Truman

Earl Warren—Chief Justice of the United States, 1970

Dr. Chaim Weitzman—Leader of World Zionists

Woodrow Wilson—28th President of the United States, 1913-1921

CHAPTER 1

WHITE HOUSE SUMMONS

At 6:00 p.m., on April 12, 1945, I returned to my Washington apartment from a Midwest assignment. As I opened the door, the phone rang. It was the White House operator with these words: "You are to come to the White House at once. Emergency!"

I rushed to my car and made for the White House. Bill Simmons, Chief Usher of the White House, met me and said, "You are to go into the Cabinet Room to swear in the new President. President Roosevelt is dead."

Although in the back of my mind there had always been the gnawing sense of this inevitability, nevertheless, when the day came, I found myself totally unprepared for the shock. I stood there for a bit, stunned and unbelieving. I was told that since Donald Nelson (who was in Roosevelt's Cabinet), was out of the city, I, as his alternate, was to sit in his place.

As I entered the Cabinet Room, I saw that the assembled Cabinet members were in a pall of deep gloom. They were awaiting the arrival of a Bible. Standing beside Vice President Truman were Chief Justice Stone and Mrs. Truman. I was led to a seat next to Henry Wallace. He seemed to be the lone person who had not surrendered to a state of despair.

Presently, I felt the arm of Wallace firmly around my shoulder. He was trying to comfort me, and there was a smile on his face. He said to me, "Dave, don't you cry. Roosevelt did not die; he was spared." Then there was a pause, and he continued. "The time had come for the Presidency of the United States to be remanded to the custody of the American people." He pointed a finger in the direction of Harry Truman and said, "And there stands the very embodiment of the American people."

When, at a later time, I shared with President Truman what Wallace had said, Truman was moved to tears. Indeed, this was a remarkable tribute to come from the man who, but for Harry Truman, might have been the one to succeed to the Presidency.

With the solemn swearing-in ceremonies over, those of us in attendance were grouped for the usual picture taking, and after offering our felicitations to the incoming President, we all began to file out. President Truman beckoned to me. I came over and he said in an undertone, "Any suggestions?"

I said that I thought the first act of the incoming President should be one of historic significance. I suggested that he send out word reaffirming the scheduled meeting in San Francisco for the drafting of a United Nations charter. President Truman nodded. It became his first decision as President.

My first meeting with Harry Truman occurred some three years before his succession to the Presidency. He was, at that time, Chairman of a Senate Committee whose responsibility was to hold to strict accountability the producers and suppliers of war materiel. The Committee soon achieved a reputation for fairness, forthrightness, and no-nonsense decisions. I was soon to become directly involved in its workings.

It was shortly after Pearl Harbor that I received an urgent call from Donald M. Nelson, Chairman of the newly set-up War Production Board, to lend a hand in overcoming some serious problems. I reported the next day at the Social Security Building in Washington, D.C., and after being sworn in, I had my first sessions with Nelson.

He was a big man physically, with the presence and bearing one might expect of the chief executive officer of Sears, Roebuck & Company. He had given up his post there to take charge of mobilizing the nation's resources for war production. We got along from the very start, and agreed on a working schedule which included an hour's private briefing each morning.

Congress had voted to give emergency control of the economy to President Roosevelt under the Second War Powers Act. This power has then redelegated to the newly-formed War Production Board (WPB) which then assumed the discretionary control over the entire American industrial complex.

The WPB became a target for any and all criticisms, claims and attacks by any special interests who felt discriminated against. Pressures came at the Board from all sides: military, labor, agriculture, consumer's groups, as well as persistent and inquisitorial hearings on the Hill. Self-interest, corporate lobbying, and power struggle became the daily refrain and routine.

On my third day with the Board, I witnessed a typical encounter on the Hill. Nelson was being subjected to rigorous cross examination by Senator Burton K. Wheeler, acting Chairman of the Senate Agricultural Committee, concerning his decision to allocate petroleum instead of grain as a source for industrial alcohol.

It was a stormy meeting. Nelson, who was an inveterate pipe smoker, would make effective use of this habit when the pressure became acute. His pipe would conveniently go out, and he would feign some difficulty in relighting it. Finally, having done so, he would take several slow puffs, turn to his inquisitor and inquire, "What was that, Mr. Senator?" Invariably, this would arrest the Senator for the moment, and it bought a little time for Nelson.

Nonetheless, the questioning continued relentlessly and probably would have gone on interminably, had it not been for the belated entrance of Senator Arthur Capper from Kansas, (the senior authority on agriculture in the Senate). In my earlier days, I had worked for Senator Capper as manager for one of his publications; it had been almost fifteen years since our last meeting. To my delight and surprise, he recognized me and greeted me warmly. He then took his place at the table, and without waiting for recognition, addressed the Committee. He had come to pay tribute to Nelson and delivered a resolution that recognized his public service at great personal sacrifice. This statement evoked from Chairman Wheeler an extended apology to Nelson and a declaration of adjournment.

Nelson showed amazing self control throughout the ordeal. He appeared calm and unruffled. However, as we were descending the stairs from the hearing room, I heard a curious squeak that seemed to be coming from his shoes. It became more pronounced as we neared his car. I stopped him and pointed to his shoes. Without a word, he raised his trouser led to reveal a veritable river of perspiration running into his shoe.

* * * *

4

Another voice had risen from the halls of Congress—a voice to reckon with—that of Harry Truman. One day Nelson showed me a letter that he had received from the newly established Truman Committee in the Senate. In that letter, Senator Truman questioned the wisdom of appointing "Dollar-a-Year" men to participate in decision making, particularly such decisions as involved the industries or companies from which they derived their compensation. Clearly this was a conflict of interest, and Truman felt that the "Dollar-a-Year" man category ought to be abolished. It was his firm belief that anyone recruited for service in the War Production Board ought to be on the government payroll, just as Chairman Nelson himself was.

Nelson viewed this as Congressional nit-picking at a time when he felt he should not divert his energies from the immense burdens of directing the WPB. He submitted the WPB's position in a letter to Senator Truman. Nelson showed me a copy of that letter. I read it with dismay, for in it Nelson brushed the Truman inquiry by invoking the Doctrine of Separation of Powers, stating that he was functioning within the Executive Branch which derived its authority from the Second War Powers Act. And then, in carefully couched legalistic terms, he dismissed the issue.

In our working relationship, Nelson knew that I would resist him when I thought he was on a wrong course. In fact, it was a condition of my acceptance of the post that I would reserve the right to speak my mind. It was obvious to me that Nelson, in his cavalier rejection of the Truman challenge, had taken the wrong turn. And, I told him so. I objected on two grounds. First, the request from Truman was clearly in the national interest. Second, it was wrong for the head of a temporary agency to assume a legal constitutional position in challenging the authority of an elected member of a permanent branch of the government. Nelson countered by saying that the time had come for him to discourage continuing Congressional intrusions on his mounting responsibilities. He disposed of the matter by saying, "What's done is done."

The more I thought about it, the more I realized that I could not let it go at that. I decided that I needed to have a visit with Senator Truman, and I took off for the Hill.

When I first saw him, I was taken aback at his unprepossessing appearance. He was in his shirtsleeves in his office on the Hill, attending to some papers, and he seemed rather ordinary. In a little while he looked up at me and said in a rather flat tone, "What can I do for you?"

"Senator, I came to see you about a letter that you wrote to Donald Nelson of the War Production Board concerning your position regarding 'Dollar-a-year-men.' In my judgement you touched on a major issue that should have had affirmative action by the Chairman, and I told him so. But regrettably, he had written a letter of nonoccurrence, and I would like to withdraw that letter." He gave me a searching look. "On whose authority are you making this request?" "My own," I said. Then, after a pause, "Do you have that authority?" I said, "No sir." Again, he looked at me intently. Then, without a word, he opened a drawer and handed me the letter.

I returned to the office, handed the letter to the Chairman, Mr. Nelson, and said, "Don, I did something that may upset you. I acted out of turn. But hear me out and you will see what I was up to." He agreed that I had acted properly and because of the importance of the work of the Truman Committee, he agreed to appear before the committee, with his "Dollar-a-year" men...and outlined their duties. Mr. Truman was pleased with this action and our friendship dated from that episode.

CHAPTER 2

THE MARSHALL PLAN

General Marshall occupied a place all his own in the esteem of Harry Truman. HST's assessment of General Marshall dated back to the time of the First World War when Truman, as Captain of Artillery, was stationed in France. Marshall was then the chief architect of the plans and tactics for the American expeditionary forces under General Pershing.

Truman and General Marshall met for the first time shortly after our involvement in World War II. Marshall was Chief of Staff of the Army, and Truman felt that he was obliged to offer himself for overseas service once again. He made some inquiries and was informed that, as a United States Senator, he would have to apply directly to General Marshall.

Truman met with Marshall and told him that he wanted to do his part by rejoining the military. Marshall, always laconic and direct, replied, "No, you're too old; we can't use you."

Truman countered, "I'm no older than you are, General."

Marshall dismissed the matter by saying, "There is a difference. I'm in!"

Marshall had a commanding presence, a keen intellect, and a rare insight into the events of history. He combined a distinguished military career with a civilian point of view, and he always stood apart from the traditional stance and projection of the military moguls. His austere mien belied a gentle and kindly disposition. General Marshall and Secretary of

War Stimson were two of the select few whom President Roosevelt entrusted with the innermost secrets of atomic development.

The work on the atomic bomb was a Herculean project. Whole new cities were built: Oakridge in Tennessee; Alamogordo in New Mexico. Some of the world's most gifted and renowned scientists and many thousands of workers were assembled—all restricted to their areas and laboring feverishly against time. The cost of the operation was running into the billions, and with the concurrent financial burden of waging war on both fronts, it naturally attracted the watchdogs of both the House and the Senate, and particularly the Truman Committee.

Congress was becoming increasingly uneasy and disturbed about being kept in the dark, and there were incipient signs of rebellion against voting such huge sums blindly. Roosevelt delegated General Marshall to plead with members of Congress not to press for a disclosure; to convince them that this was an extremely sensitive and unprecedented undertaking; and to make clear that if the slightest hint of what it was about should reach the enemies' ears, it would deprive us of the element of surprise. Finally, he said, "I plead with you to take my word for it that this is a matter which we must keep under wraps for the duration. It is absolutely hush hush."

Marshall, who possessed the highest reputation for credibility and statesmanship, was taken at his word, and the Congress pressed no further. Truman, too, was persuaded by Marshall's plea, and for the first time did not pursue a matter scheduled for an investigation by his committee. It should be noted that even after Truman became Vice President, he still was not privy to any information about the development of the atomic bomb—so tight was the mantle of secrecy.

A central command for the European theater to plan the Normandy Invasion was being set up. Winston Churchill requested that Roosevelt assign General Marshall to that command. But, Roosevelt told him that he could not, under any circumstances, spare him because the American efforts against a stubborn and fanatical enemy on the Pacific Front depended heavily on Marshall's tactical brilliance. Instead, Roosevelt appointed General Eisenhower to that post, and he assured Churchill that Ike would fill the role ably. Ike did and, of course, Marshall distinguished himself in the Pacific.

From the day that Truman came to the Presidency, he planned to make use of Marshall's talents in a high cabinet post. In 1947, when James F. Byrnes left his post as Secretary of State, Truman had his opportunity. However, there was a barrier that had to be negotiated. By regulation and tradition, only a civilian could be Secretary of State. But, such was Marshall's reputation and record of achievement that Congress quickly voted a special dispensation, and for the first time a top military man occupied the office of Secretary of State.

When the General took command of the Department of State, he sought to impose his own administrative style and tempo, and lost no time in issuing certain edicts. Among them was the order that all documents or communications were to be dispatched in the mail pouch on the same day that he signed them. He soon discovered that he was up against a tradition-bound, time-encrusted labyrinth whose procedures were impossible for him to alter. Other Secretaries of State before and since Marshall were similarly frustrated by entrenched functionaries.

In order to cut through this kind of bureaucratic intransigency, President Roosevelt found it necessary to make use of Harry Hopkins as his direct personal representative. Before him, Woodrow Wilson had to designate Colonel E. M. House to bypass traditional channels. More recently, President Nixon circumvented the State Department in creating a special post for Henry Kissinger in the White House. But not so with Harry Truman. He shunned intermediaries and worked directly with Secretary of State Marshall on a daily basis.

Origin of the Marshall Plan

The genesis of the Marshall Plan traces back to the final months of the Roosevelt Administration. The Nelson White House unit was charged with the development of a program to deal with postwar European reconstruction. In a report to President Roosevelt headed "Responsibility of the Major Power to the Junior Nations," the Nelson Group recommended that a pilot program be underwritten to help in the restoration of Greece and one Balkan nation, either Czechoslovakia or Yugoslavia. From these preliminary efforts we would gain the experience necessary to formulate a more comprehensive plan. This recommendation received President Roosevelt's approval.

After Roosevelt's death, this plan was brought to President Truman's attention. He considered it carefully, but it did not satisfy him because it fell short of the mark. He had been thinking in broader terms. This kind of a pilot operation, although a sound, logical first step, would involve needless delay. Truman wanted a comprehensive plan that could be applied quickly to meet the crisis, and he submitted recommendations to the State Department.

The Department got to work on it with a special sense of urgency and came up with an outline that contained essentially the thinking of the President. At the time when the plan was developed to its final stage, President Truman was scheduled to make a speech in Cleveland, Mississippi, on May 8, 1947. But, because of commitments planned for his birthday on that date, he asked Undersecretary of State Dean Acheson to take the platform in his place. The key points were predicated on the hypothesis that peace and freedom from want were interrelated and that our own democratic institutions would benefit from the economic interplay of stable and prosperous nations.

This speech was the forerunner of the famous one delivered by Secretary of State Marshall one month later on June 5th at a Harvard University commencement where Marshall was to get an honorary degree. The speech received instant acclaim, and the following morning the press had already dubbed it the "Marshall Plan."

President Truman couldn't have been more pleased at this tribute, and he derived particular pleasure when it brought Marshall the Nobel Prize for Peace. This subject came up while I was working with President Truman on the preparation of his "Memoirs." The President looked at me intently and said, "No one could have been more deserving than he."

GEORGE C. MARSHALL

by Harry S. Truman

General Marshall was one of the most astute and profound men I have ever known. He possessed that rare gift of getting to the heart of a problem at almost the instant he faced it. Yet he was a patient man. He talked very little, but listened carefully to everyone who had anything to say. I recall his sitting for an hour or more with little or no expression on his face-and then come up with a comment that would cut to the bone of the matter under discussion.

He held a post of the highest responsibility in the Roosevelt Administration and I called on his great capacity as a leader in assigning him to many difficult postwar tasks-including one that was impossible of solution-the exasperating and frustrating mission to China.

When the situation in China in 1946 indicated serious trouble from the Communists, we were in position to send the kind of military force that would insure control by Chiang Kai-Shek. The only thing we could do was to attempt to exert whatever influence we could to prevent civil war. The man for this job had to possess exceptional qualities of skill and patience. There was only one such man for so demanding an undertaking-General Marshall.

But General Marshall had just turned over his duties as Chief of Staff of the Army to General Eisenhower, and no man had earned the right to a restful and honorable retirement than did Marshall. Yet I knew no one else with capacity to meet this critical situation with such vast implications to the future of the world.

So I went to the telephone in the Red Room of the White House and called the General in his home in Leesburg, Virginia. I came right to the point and said: "General, I want you to go to China for me." Marshall replied, "Yes, Mr. President" and hung up abruptly.

When General Marshall came to the White House two days later to discuss his mission, I asked him why he had hung up on me without asking any questions. He then told me that he and Mrs. Marshall had just driven up to the house when my call came though, and he wanted to spare her the shock of how short lived this vacation was to be, especially when she was so worried about his health. He expected to break the news to her gently-but when they turned on their radio some minutes later there was a bulletin announcing the General's mission. "There was the devil to pay," he admitted.

As Secretary of State, Marshall had to listen to more staff talk than when he was Chief of Staff. Here again he would listen for a long time without comment, but when the debates between the members of his staff seemed as if they would go on endlessly, he would suddenly cut in and say, "Gentlemen, don't fight the problem, decide it."

Dean Acheson told me a characteristic story about Marshall when he first took over as Secretary of State. Marshall had asked Acheson to stay on as Under Secretary and said, "I want the most complete and blunt truths from you, particularly about myself. And Dean Acheson replied, "Do you, General?" "Yes" Marshall said. "I have no feeling excepting a few which I reserve for Mrs. Marshall."

When Secretary Marshall returned from the Moscow Conference of Foreign Ministers, he was in a pessimistic mood. He had hoped he could persuade the Russians that the United States was working for peace. The Russians, on the other hand, were interested only in their own plans and were coldly determined to exploit the miserable conditions of Europe to establish Communism there-rather than cooperate with the West in the interest of peace.

Marshall's report confirmed my conviction that there was no time to lose in finding a way to save Europe. In a speech by Acheson at Cleveland, Mississippi-and a proposal later made by Marshall on June 5, 1947 at Harvard our plan for dealing with the European crisis was evolved-and the "Marshall Plan" was launched.

I began to refer to the plan for the revival of Europe in the White House staff meetings as the "Marshall Plan" because I wanted him to get full credit for his brilliant contributions to the measure which he helped to formulate-for it was he who had envisioned the full scope of the economic rescue program. He had perceived not only the inspirational but the economic value of the proposal as well.

History, I am certain will always associate the name of Marshall with this program which helped save Europe from economic disaster-and enslavement by Russian Communism.

Marshall was one of the few men in the government who was in intimate contact with the day-to-day developments of this country's wartime operations in both hemispheres.

As a military strategist and as a diplomat he was known and respected abroad as few men have been in the history of the United States. At home

General Marshall enjoyed the confidence and esteem of the average citizen regardless of political preferences. He enjoyed the admiration and respect of both houses of Congress and his judgment carried great weight- and his personality inspired confidence with those with whom he dealt.

I recall the worried and anxious months of the early part of 1944, before the Normandy invasion. There were many men in Congress who had misgivings about the cross-channel attack. General Marshall came to the Capital and spoke to about four hundred of us in his quiet, determined manner. His complete command of all the facts of the situation soon quieted whatever fears anyone may have had. His many years in Washington in wartime provided him with a thorough knowledge of the role of Congress-and as head of the Army he had to deal with administrative problems of unprecedented magnitude and he performed brilliantly.

The people of the United States, indeed the people of all nations who prize their freedom, are fortunate to have had a man of his great stature and many gifts in their service during so dangerous a period in their history.

He was invaluable to me as friend and colleague. I was overcome with sadness when I was informed of his passing-and I thereupon expressed my estimation of this giant among men in the following public statement.

(Following statement issued on Oct. 20, 1959 in Washington, D.C.)

My friends—friends of General Marshall.

General Marshall was an honorable man, a truthful man, a man of ability.

Honor has no modifying adjectives—a man has it or he hasn't. General Marshall had it.

Truth has no qualifying words to be attached to it. A man either tells the truth or he doesn't. General Marshall was the exemplification of the men of truth.

Ability can be qualified. Some of us have little of it, some may have moderate ability, and some men have it to the extreme. General Marshall was a man of the greatest ability.

He was the greatest general since Robert E. Lee.

He was the greatest administrator since Thomas Jefferson.

He was the man of honor, the man of truth, the man of greatest ability.

He was the greatest of the great in our time.

I sincerely hope that when it comes my time to cross the great river General Marshall will place me on his staff so that I may try to do for him what he did for me.

Harry Truman

CHAPTER 3

TRUMAN AND ACHESON

Dean Acheson was endowed with a commanding presence. He was tall, erect and aristocratic, with piercing eyes, and bushy eyebrows. He exercised a sharp tongue. In his highly sensitive post as Secretary of State, he frequently put adversaries to rout by the very force of his logic and eloquence.

However, his appearances before Senate Committees often tried his patience and, at time, his manners. He gave the impression of talking down his nose to the members of Congress with veiled contempt. Acheson was asked one day by a colleague why his performances before congressional committees were so patronizing. His explanation was, "It is perhaps because I cannot conceal my contempt for the contemptible."

His fiery temper often struck terror in those who would contest him. With all that, he could be very accommodating, very charming, very persuasive. These talents which brought him national renown as one of the gifted members of the bar were put to effective use in his service to the government.

For example, Acheson presided over a meeting in San Francisco at which John Foster Dulles, who had just returned from his mission to Japan where he negotiated the post-war treaty, spoke. It was a triumphal moment for Dulles as he, with incisive clarity, outlined the treaty, word for word, line for line, paragraph by paragraph. It was evident that a major treaty had been negotiated in the interest of both nations.

Some aspects of the treaty were undergoing discussion during the question period that followed. Gromyko, speaking for Soviet Russia whose entry into the war against Japan was a bit belated, launched a diatribe in an obvious attempt to becloud and downgrade the treaty. That display of diversionary tactics provoked Acheson to deflate Gromyko to an uncomfortable level. Gromyko had met his master, and for him it turned out to be a shattering and painful experience.

When the session ended, everyone present could not help but be impressed with the performance of Dean Acheson; he was totally in control throughout. As for John Foster Dulles, who had acquitted himself so ably in his presentation of the treaty, when it came to ad libbing, he was on less firm ground, and his response was halting and equivocal.

At my next meeting with the President, I gave him my impression of the San Francisco meeting. He had a ready explanation for me when I expressed my disappointment at Dulles' lackluster ad libbing. "Dulles," he said, "is a high powered lawyer and a very skillful negotiator, but you have to write it all out for him. When you sent him on a mission, you have to arm him with a detailed brief."

Under Roosevelt, Acheson had held the post of Undersecretary of the Treasury. He attracted a measure of prominence in that position. At that critical time, in order to meet the monetary crises, Roosevelt moved boldly to take the nation off the gold standard. He did so without consulting with Dean Acheson. It so happened that Acheson stubbornly held to the principle of gold as indispensable to a sound monetary system. He telephoned Roosevelt to lodge his protest and presented his views. Roosevelt was not dissuaded. Whereupon, Acheson tendered his resignation which was promptly accepted.

In the light of that experience, how did it come to pass that Acheson, who was unable to find common ground in his association with the Roosevelt Administration, would find himself in tune and accord with President Truman? People in and out of government had expressed wonderment as to how these two men—the matter of fact, direct, no nonsense man from Missouri, and the high powered, aristocratic, intellectual Acheson—found themselves in a close working relationship.

I had occasion to observe the two men together and often marveled at the degree of accommodation that Acheson always exhibited when in the presence of President Truman. Acheson was deferential, not only to the office, but to the man in the White House, yet he was never submissive and never failed to express himself freely in the shaping of all decisions. It was an ideal working arrangement, unique in the conduct of American foreign policy.

Years later, when I was interviewing him for the Truman memoirs, Acheson himself revealed, with striking candor, how it all came about. Acheson came to our offices in the Federal Reserve Bank Building in Kansas City for the interview, and it was a happy reunion between him and the President. HST escorted Acheson into my office where we were joined by the President's personal secretary, Rose Conway. The President having departed, we proceeded with the interview.

At first, Acheson seemed rather tense and required his pipe and some refreshment to put him at ease. I opened the interview with this question:

"Mr. Secretary, there is no need for me to point out to you the importance of this interview. Whatever you will have to say is to go into the archives as a permanent record in order that future chroniclers of this period will have an authentic source from which to base their judgments. In a sense, we are dealing here with the record of the Truman Administration and your significant contributions to it. For a starter, let's open with a question which has been on many minds. How is it possible for an aristocratic intellectual such as you to find common ground with a pedestrian farmer from Missouri, Harry Truman?"

Acheson put his pipe down and looked at me very searchingly, "You must be joking!"

I said, "No, sir. It's a question that needs to be answered for the record, and you are the one to clear it up."

Acheson said, "Without President Truman to back me up and to sustain me, I could have achieved precious little."

"That's a revealing comment, Mr. Secretary. Would you mind expanding on it?" I asked.

"Perhaps then," he said, "I should go back to the beginning. Shortly after his re-election, President Truman called me to the White House to discuss a decision he was about to make. This is how the President approached the matter. "Dean, I am about to appoint you as Secretary of State." Then he looked at me intently and continued. "But, you will not be President, and I will not be Secretary of State. This is how we will work this out together. All important decisions will be made in this office. I don't want you to come in at 5 o'clock in the afternoon with a decision that has to be transmitted by 6:00 p.m. that same day. That will not do, for you will be confronting me with a decision already made, and that gives me no opportunity to consider the matter. I also want it understood that when you come to me with an important policy recommendation, I would like to have you bring along those in the department who are opposed to the recommendation, as I would want to hear them out, too.'"

Acheson cited a number of illustrations which he considered illustrative of his working relationships with the President. One such instance took place when he made an appearance before a Senate Committee on an issue currently in the news. He was subjected to grueling questioning concerning his method of dealing with the mounting threat of Communism. When the questioning verged upon the accusative, and the chairman went so far as to insinuate that Acheson was tending to be soft on Communism, all restraint went out of him and he blurted out, "Senator, if that's how you feel about it, make the most of it."

At that point, the newsmen rushed for the telephones. This was a sensational development. Acheson realized at once that he had committed a serious blunder. He gathered up his papers and in a frustrated mood, walked back to his office. As he approached the State Department Building, he passed a newsstand on which there were already newspapers with screaming headlines: "Acheson Soft on Communism, Committee Charges!" Acheson was now certain that his usefulness had come to an end, and that there was only one course of action open to him. When he got to his office, he picked up his personal papers, marched over to the White House, and asked to see the President on a matter of personal urgency. In short order he was invited into the Oval Office where the

President received him cordially, as always. The President then asked casually, "What is the problem, Dean?"

Acheson replied, "I came to tender my resignation which I wish you to accept forthwith. I have committed an egregious blunder at a Senate hearing this morning which renders me useless as Secretary of State."

The President didn't seem to be impressed or upset at this dramatic declaration. He simply lifted a slip of paper from the ticker tape, handed it matter of factly to Acheson, saying, "Is that what is troubling you, Dean?"

"Yes, Mr. President, and don't you think that is quite enough?"

The President said, "Dean, one more headline like this and you will make a damn good Secretary of State."

The role of a Secretary of State is fraught with unremitting pressure. No matter what he says, or how he acts, there always will be some group, some element of our society that will take umbrage and bombard him with criticism. Ofttimes such charges find expression on the floor of the House or in the Senate. Thus, when a Secretary of State, to whom full authority is delegated by a President, finds himself on the defensive, he is obliged to divert much of his time and energies in defending his positions. Whereas, when a President retains to himself his Constitutional authority to make foreign policy decisions, and in certain circumstances with the advice and consent of the Senate, then his Secretary of State acts as his representative in effectuating that policy.

During the period of the Truman Administration, that is how the Secretary of State and the President worked in close association. It was a time of new and imaginative foreign policy decisions. Much of the war devastation was repaired. The fallen enemies were helped not only in the restoration of their nations, but in the transition toward rejoining the world community.

All of this embraced the Truman concept of the American role of leading the world into a synergic effort for peace as the ultimate goal. With the coming of the nuclear age, uppermost in Truman's mind was the survival of mankind. It needs to be recorded that Secretary of State Dean Acheson applied his many talents in working tirelessly towards building that kind of world.

History has shown us that no matter how enlightened a foreign policy may be, or how strong a Secretary of State is, there is little chance of success if the nation is lead by a weak President. When that condition occurs, the constitutional responsibility for the making of foreign policy by the President is not merely delegated to the Secretary of State but, in fact, relegated to him.

Acheson then went on to cite how he lived through another crisis that threatened his survival in office. This had to do with the bizarre Alger Hiss, Whittaker Chambers pumpkin papers intrigue. Richard Nixon, a then obscure member of the Lower House, was in the role of investigator/prosecutor. Clearly, Hiss was vulnerable, and his exposure occurred at a time when the nation was quick to react to Communist sympathizers or Communist collaborators. It was a situation made to order to feed the political ambitions of Congressman Nixon. He made the most of it. It catapulted him into national attention and transformed him into a man with political promise.

In the wake of this development and in the climate in which it occurred, the press took aim on Secretary Acheson. Let Secretary Acheson take it from here: "I contemplated my press conference with misgivings and anxiety. My wife and I sat up much of the night in an effort to focus in on the morning's press conference, and how I would respond to Alger Hiss revelations. My wife, who sat knitting, kept insisting that she could be of no help to me, that this was my personal decision, and that I alone would have to make it.

"The fact is that the more I thought of it, the less sense I could make of it. And, in that condition, I dropped off to sleep. I slept fitfully.

"I arrived at the press conference without having the slightest idea of what I was going to say. As I expected, the press conference opened with the one question to which I did not have a clear answer. 'What do you intend to do about Alger Hiss now?' I responded with what I hoped would be a quotably diverting phrase, 'I never turn my back on a friend.' Even before I finished the sentence, I knew that I was in trouble. I should have said anything but that, but it was too late to undo it. The irony of this whole inadvertence is that Alger Hiss, by no stretch of the imagination, could be regarded as a personal friend. We had very little contact, and what there was could only have been casual. I knew of no reason to be protective of him.

"But, having said it, it was out. Being out, it found its way quickly into the headlines of the newspapers, and once again I was in a crisis. Again I assembled my personal belongings from my desk, walked over to the White House, and asked to see the President.

"I received his usual broad smile which I was in no mood to return. The President asked, 'Is there some kind of trouble, Dean?' I replied, 'Mr. President, I came away from a press conference where I blurted out a statement that was so inept and personally compromising that I see no possible way that I can continue. I would appreciate it if we did not go into any discussion of it. My resolution is final.'

"Without a word, the President handed me the note on his desk containing the quotation. Then he said, 'Dean, sit down. You're talking to the man who attended the funeral of a criminal friend of his because he thought it was the right thing to do. I have received a great deal of abuse and criticism because of that act, but I felt it was a personal obligation. Now, you have no cause to be upset or disturbed. Never mind the barbs and the brickbats. You and I have important work to do.' That was the last time I ever had reason to bring up the subject or resignation."

This remarkable association between a President who performed such an historic role in reshaping the post-war world, and his Secretary of State who helped bring it to fruition with such great negotiating skill, accounts for one of the brightest chapters in American foreign policy.

Truman ranked Acheson second only to Jefferson as one of our greatest Secretaries of State. In their long association involving the many historic decisions, there was never a dichotomy except in the matter concerning the recognition of the State of Israel. Acheson had strong views concerning the eruptive nature of that part of the world, and he wanted no involvement.

After his tenure of office, Acheson gave expression to his own views. He tended to shift to a hawkish posture which received considerable attention in the press. This, however, in no way impaired the deep bond between Truman and Acheson, except that it did serve to point up the creative source of America's world peace program.

The following is a message from Dean Acheson to Mr. Truman in which Dean Acheson unburdens himself to HST in a devastating historical critique—restricted to posthumous release.

"The message which you and Mrs. Truman sent me was most kind and thoughtful of you, as have always been to me. My brother, who was ten years younger than I, died very suddenly, as he was reading at home. He had no history of heart trouble, though he had been in poor shape for some years from progressive emphysema. One of his proudest memories was of holding the title of your "Personal Representative" in late '47 or '48 when John Hilldring sent him off to Scandinavia to buy fish for the Germans to eat on Fridays-Now I am the only one left of my generation in the family, although I was the oldest.

We had hoped to go to an Army dinner in honor of you and were saddened to get word that the Boss had wisely decided to save your energy for other things. It is too long since we have seen you. I do hope that you are coming back strongly from your illness.

This year I put in five months of what Lincoln called "unrequired toil" in the State Department for J and R on the DeGaulle-NATO crisis. I found it-between you and me-a most disillusioning experience in regard to both men. I recommended R to K when he wanted to appoint, of all people, F,; and had high hopes of him. He had been a good assistant to me, loyal and capable. But as number one he has been no good at all. For some reason, unknown to me he will not disclose his mind to anyone. The Dept. is totally at a loss to know what he wants done or what he thinks. All sorts of channels spring up between various people in the dept. and WH aides which result in conflicting policies getting rumored about.

L is not much better. He, too, hates to decide matters, is a worse postponer (sic) of decisions than R. The phrase for that now is "to preserve all one's options." That means to drift and let decisions be made by default. It passes for statesmanship in our town today.

Two other things about J. He can't carry on more than a few matters at once. Now a days his preoccupations are Vietnam and the balance of payments-So Europe is forgotten and a good deal that you, GM and I did is unraveling fast. For the Chief of the world's greatest power and the only one capable of world responsibility. This is disaster. The other is that he is not only devious but would rather be devious than straight forward. While I was doing my best to advise him on NATO, and while he was writing message and making speeches I wrote for him, he was circulating rumors in the press that my views were not his. If they were not a half hours talk could have gotten us together. But it was not until I blew up that we had it and then I never did find out what he wanted done differently.

At any rate, I am now a free man, writing a book about my years in the SD [and] about another President who used to do things very differently.

It is really too bad about J. He could do so much better than he is. He creates distrust by being too smart. He is never quite candid. He is both mean and generous but the meanness too often predominates. He yields to petty impulses such as the desire to surprise everyone with every appointment. It is too childish.

Well, I have gotten a lot off my chest.

Alice who is blooming (can you believe that we shall have been married 50 years next May!) Sends her love to you and B, as do I-

As ever, Dean

Joe Alsop and his brother, Stewart, were Eastern Establishment groomed newspaper reporters on the Washington scene during much of the Truman administration. They made it very clear, whenever they appeared, that they were well born, came from good stock, did things right and you better believe it. Like Franklin D. Roosevelt, they had little regard or patience with this "dirt farmer" from Missouri— "this hick," "this rube"—and did not hesitate to make this clear in their columns. The attitude was common in many so-called cultural circles but it never bothered Harry Truman.

They were good reporters for their time occasionally making themselves insufferable by using their connections, starting with Heaven, the White House, and anywhere else they could pull a string. Thus this letter of apology from Joe Alsop is quite astonishing but not surprising for he did have a head on his shoulders. It is also quite revealing as to the depth of their intelligence in dealing with world leaders which they prattled about in their columns. Harry Truman took it in stride, as he did everything, and replied in simple Missouri fashion. In this instance which was followed up by David Noyes and Dean Acheson, there was little substance to the story by Joe Alsop.

2805 P Street

Washington, D. C.

Dear Boss,

Will you please get Mr. Noyes to help me in a matter I want to fight to correct an error which Joe Alsop has now printed four times about you. I enclose his last rendition of it today. I think better of Joe than you once did-I remember your references to Alsop-but unless firmly corrected he will go on repeating error until people begin to believe it.

Paul Nitze and I, having compared notes are sure that you never sent a standstill order to Ridgeway. To accuse you of causing 90,000 needless casualties two needless years of war is outrageous.

I am asking Bradley to search his memory and papers about this and also Joe Collins. Paul will have a search made in the Pentagon. Will you ask Noyes to see whether your papers show anything on the subject. I don't want to quote anybody or any paper. I only want to assert on my authority that after inquiries which convince one that I know the facts that you issued no standstill order in connection with any armistice talks nor interfered in any way with military operations at that time. You followed at all times your normal relations with the Joint Chiefs of Staff and the Secretary of State and of Defense.

These columnists try to rewrite history as much as the communists.

I hate to bother you with this, but I do think that it is important not to let this repeated misstatement to continue without correction.

Alice sends love to you both.

All your successors demonstrate what rugged health you had—yet you were never paid for overtime.

Affectionately,

/s/ Dean

November 21, 1966

Dear Dean:

I have no idea where or from whom Alsop could have picked up the notion of a standstill order or how he came to make the ugly charge in his column. It was bad enough when you and I had to put up with this sort of thing in the days when it was our responsibility - but to use it now in relation to the Viet Nam situation is a little hard to take.

Dave has dug up some passages from the documents which may help. We tried to reach Bob Dennison but he is out of the country. Sid Souers suggested that the most likely source for a final check would be Omar Bradley.

Bess joins me in sending you and Alice our best.

Sincerely yours,

Honorable Dean Acheson
2805 P Street, N. W.
Washington, D. C.

33

November 21, 1966

MEMORANDUM TO: The President

FROM: David Noyes

An over the week-end search of the documents in your personal files failed to produce anything that could possibly give credence to the assertion by Joseph Alsop that you had issued a standstill order to Ridgway either prior to or during the Armistice negotiations with the Communists in Korea-or at any other time. I checked with Admiral Sidney Souers, who was at that time your consultant on security matters, and Sid was positive that there was no standstill order.

There is much evidence to the contrary as shown by the following excerpts from the documents:

MacArthur Hearings-May 8, 1951

Marshall said that there was a "very real possibility" of Soviet intervention in the Korean War. In such circumstances, he said, the U. S. would be forced into action against the Soviet Union, but Marshall added that such action had been avoidable up to the present. He said that he could recall <u>no instance</u> in which Truman had overruled his military advisers in behalf of a position taken by the Department of State.

June 1951

General Van Fleet announced on June 2 that the "Pursuit phase" of the campaign had been ended with the clearing of the enemy from South

Korea (except in the west). He said that U. N. forces would conduct operations in North Korea "when necessary and profitable." In accordance with this policy, he immediately launched an offensive against the "iron triangle" on the central front.

From HST Speech-July 1951

Addressing 60,000 people in Cadillac Square in Detroit, President Truman said that we did not know whether the enemy really wanted peace in Korea or whether "they are simply trying to gain by negotiations what they have not been able to gain by conquest."

From: General Ridgeway To: President Truman
(July 4, 1951)

In mid June counterattacking United Nations ground forces were meeting increased resistance as noted in the previous report. As United Nations forces reached and occupied their main objectives, hostile forces from organized positions opposed advances with determination. United Nations patrols ranged forward of the main battle position to maintain firm contact, but relatively little aggressive action has been undertaken by either side.

On the western part of the front from Changdan to Kumhwa, United Nations combat patrols found the enemy alert, well organized, and determined. Along this 50 mile arc, the enemy appears to have achieved a considerable measure of defensive organization, consisting of well developed earthworks, and a well integrated series of anti-tank defenses covering the main approaches, including elaborate tank traps, roadblocks and minefields.

On the 35 mile portion of the central front extending from Kumhwa to the vicinity of Pia, hostile troops clung tenaciously to positions in the immediate vicinity of the United Nations lines throughout the period. Contacts were particularly frequent on A 12 mile sector from Kumhwa to Hudong. There the enemy displayed great sensitivity, stoutly resisted United Nations probing, and himself engaged in numerous small unit probing efforts and moderate strength counterattacks. Due north of this front along the Kumsong Changdo axis, sightings reveal that a rather extensive hostile build up is in progress. Significant is a growing network of dumps and other supply installations established well forward, many within 5 miles of the United Nations front lines.

<u>From: General Ridgway To: President Truman</u>

(July 10, 1951)

(Quote from Senior United Nations Command Delegate, Vice Admiral Charles Turner Joy)

"It is understood, of course, that hostilities will continue in all areas, except in those neutral zones agreed upon, until such time as there is an agreement on the terms governing the armistice and until such time as an approved Armistice Commission is prepared to function. The United Nations Command Delegation is prepared to do its part in trying to work out an armistice agreement with the representatives of the Communist

Forces in Korea, for the cessation of hostilities in Korea, under conditions which will assure against their resumption.

<u>From: General Ridgway to: President Truman</u>
(July 17, 1951)
(Quote from Vice Admiral Joy-this was in July 10 memorandum also)

"It is understood, of course, that hostilities will continue in all areas except in those neutral zones agreed upon, until such time as there is an agreement on the terms governing the armistice and until such time as an approved armistice commission is prepared to function.

<u>From: Joint Chiefs of Staff   To: President Truman</u>
Paragraph G
(Corrected and Improved by HST)

There must be no relaxation in military effort on our part until proper arrangements for cessation of hostilities have been agreed upon as contained in the armistice terms.

****

JOSEPH WRIGHT ALSOP
2810 DUMBARTON AVENUE
WASHINGTON, D. C.

March 12, 1965

Dear Mr President:

On advice of counsel --- the very best that
cannot be hired ---- I write you this letter with
some trepidation. I asked Dean Acheson whether
it would merely strike you as ridiculously presumptuous or would please you. He said, very
sensibly, that it might indeed strike you as
presumptuous but that he thought it would also
please you.

My purpose is simply to apologize for the
inexperience and bad judgment which led me to
underrate your leadership of our country while
you were in office. When I look back now, I must
say with greater opportunities for comparison,
your years in the White House seem to me a truly

heroic period. Nowadays, I never lose a chance
to say that in print. But I did not say it then,
and that is why I think an apology is owed.

Sincerely & Respectfully

March 19, 1965

Dear Mr. Alsop:

Indeed, you could not have pleased me more. Nor
need you have felt that you would be presuming in
writing me on any subject.

It is true that I did not always react pleasantly to
criticism - or derisive comments - but I never for
a moment questioned the right of anyone to do so.

But there is something in my make-up that rebels
at the thought of exacting an apology from any who
has disapproved of me - and I surely would not
expect to receive one from so talented an observer
as yourself.

But I warmly welcome your reassessment of the
period and dare hope that it might be sustained by
the ultimate judgment.

Sincerely yours,

Mr. Joseph Wright Alsop
2720 Dumbarton Avenue
Washington, D. C.

CHAPTER 4

START OF THE CIA

Almost from the day that Truman assumed the Presidency, he began to feel the inadequacy of intelligence summaries that came to his desk, and the discrepancies of the assessments they contained. He intended to correct the situation as soon as the problems generated by the way were out of the way. By the middle of 1946, the President inaugurated plans for the establishment of a central intelligence facility that would assemble vital and pertinent information that would reach his desk unevaluated, unslanted, and undoctored. He wanted it raw and unedited, for it struck him that some of the reports he received from the various agencies were contradictory. In other words, the Department of Defense might have one conclusion, the Department of State another, the Treasury still another, and when they were summarized and presented to the President, they did not always reflect the true state of affairs.

In order for him to be accurately and fully informed in the decision making process, Truman decided that he had to make certain that the intelligence information that reached him was based on facts and not assumptions and deductions. He thereupon established a special unit whose prime responsibility would be to gather all basic intelligence from the various departments of the government engaged in intelligence work. With the aid of such a facility, the President could be better served in arriving at sound judgments. That is how and why the CIA came into being. It was not intended to supersede the existing agencies assigned to intelligence work; rather it would be the clearinghouse for all the information that was collected.

For a time everything went well, and the agency was functioning as it was designed to do under its director, Admiral Sidney Souers in adhering strictly to its function. But soon Congress took note of this new intelligence facility and decided to expand it into a major intelligence gathering organization. It enacted legislation putting this agency into the business of foreign intelligence and all the concomitants that go with it. They allocated vast amounts to be used at its sole discretion with only perfunctory accountability to a special Congressional committee.

President Truman regretted this action by the Congress. He even went so far as to counsel Allen Dulles (its new director) to eschew this operation order to save himself from possible embarrassment and criticism. However, by that time, Dulles was already completely involved in the far flung activities of the agency and found this new role to his liking. As the CIA had become our super intelligence agency restricted to the foreign field, the FBI concurrently became limited to domestic operations. It should be said that the CIA, by its charter, was preempted from any activities in the continental United States.

Through his administration, the CIA exhibited a measure of restraint, but HST was still uncomfortable about so vast and so amply financed an organization turned loose upon a world fraught with suspicion. Later, when the activities of the CIA had brought upon it the castigation of the world press, our enemies were presented with an effective propaganda weapon with which to impugn the United States. It would have been preferable if the KGB had sustained sole monopoly in that kind of operation.

The propaganda mills of our detractors had reached such a fever pitch of intensity that Truman could no longer restrain himself. He deemed it his duty to restate the original purpose for which the CIA was founded. He published an article on December 22, 1963, as part of his syndicated series.

THE CIA...AS I KNEW IT

by Harry S. Truman

I think it has become necessary to take another look at the purpose and operations of our Central Intelligence Agency...The CIA. At least I would like to submit here the original reason why I thought it necessary to organize this agency during my administration, what I expected it to do, and how it was to operate as an arm of the President.

I think it is fairly obvious that by and large a President's performance in office is as effective as the information he has and the information he gets. That is to say, that assuming the President himself possesses a knowledge of our history, a sensitive understanding of our institutions and an insight into the needs and aspirations of the people, he needs to have available to him the most accurate and up to the minute information on whatever is going on everywhere in the world and particularly of the trends and developments in all the danger spots in the contest between East and West. This is an immense task and requires a special kind of intelligence facility.

Of course, every President has available to him all the information gathered by the many intelligence agencies already in existence. The Department of State Defense, Commerce, Interior, and others are constantly engaged in extensive information gathering and have done excellent work.

But their collective information reached the President all too frequently in conflicting conclusions. At times the intelligence reports tended to be shaped to conform with the established positions of a given department thus becoming confusing and what's worse did not contribute to making a firm decision.

Therefore I decided to set up a special organization charged with the collection of all intelligence reports from every available source and to have them reach me as President without departmental treatment or interpretation.

I wanted and needed the information in its natural raw state and in as comprehensive a volume as was practical for me to make full use of it. But the most important thing about this move was to guard against any chance of intelligence being used to influence or to lead the President into unwise decisions. And I thought it was necessary that the President do his own thinking and evaluation.

The CIA has been diverted from its original assignment for it has become a policy making arm of the government. This has led to trouble and may have compounded our difficulties in several explosive areas.

I never had any thought when I set up the CIA that it would be injected into peacetime cloak and dagger operations. Some of the complications and embarrassments which I think we have experienced are in part attributable to the fact that the quiet intelligence arm of the President has been so removed from its intended role that it is being interpreted as a symbol of sinister and mysterious foreign intrigue. And a subject for cold war enemy propaganda.

With all the nonsense put out by the Communist propaganda about: "Yankee Imperialism" and "Exploitive Capitalism," "War Mongers," "Monopolists" in their name calling about the West, the last thing we needed was that the CIA to be seized upon as something being used to subvert influence in the affairs of a free people.

I well knew the temporary first Director of the CIA, Admiral Souers, and the later permanent director, General Hoyt Vanderberg, and Allen Dulles. These were men of the highest character, patriotism, and integrity and I assume that is all those who continue in charge.

But there are now some searching questions which have to be answered and I would like to see the CIA assume its original assignment as the intelligence arm of the President.

We have grown up as a nation well known for our free institutions and for our ability to maintain a free and open society. There is something about the way the CIA operates that is casting a huge shadow over our country.

December 22, 1963 (David Noyes)

Following the publication of Truman's critical commentary on the CIA, I received a call from an old acquaintance in charge of the CIA outpost in Geneva. He took umbrage at the nature of the Truman critique and averred that the operations of the CIA were conducted along the accepted traditions of such institutions. I told him that he was addressing himself to the wrong person. It was President Truman who had signed the birth certificate of that agency, and it was he who had clearly defined its purpose. What had developed over the years was at variance with his concept and intent, and its current activities were putting the nation in a bad light. We had labored, as a nation, long and hard and made many great sacrifices, for which we had earned the respect of the free world, and nothing should be permitted to put it in jeopardy.

The caller protested that assessment and went on to say that no one in the CIA would knowingly do anything that would in any way tend to discredit the United States. I told him that I thought he was obviously reading the wrong papers, and for a man engaged in his discipline, he was curiously out of touch.

This is how President Truman expressed his misgivings about the CIA to me.

Dec 1, 63

When I took over :—

The President had no means of coordinating the intelligence from around the world nor from the United States, Alaska, Puerto Rica, Hawaii and the Philipines.

The State Dept., Defense Dept., Atty. General: Dept., Commerce, Agriculture, Interior and all the Departments had connextions abroad. They had to be coordinated and I decided on a Central Intelligence Agency to do just that. It worked when I had control. It was not intended as a "Cloak & Dagger Outfit"!

It was intended merely as a center for keeping the President informed on what was going on in the world at large and the United States and its dependencies in particular.

It should not be an agency to initiate policy or to act as a spy organization. That was never the intention when it was organized.

CHAPTER 5

ATOM BOMB

The intransigence of the Japanese military command was convincingly demonstrated, even after the fall of Okinawa—a victory so decisive as to prove the futility of further resistance. In winning the battle of Okinawa, we had sustained frightful losses. The sum total of our casualties in all of our services included over 4900 sailors killed or missing in action, and over 4800 wounded; 7613 soldiers killed or missing in action, and 31,800 wounded; the Navy lost 34 vessels, with 368 damaged.

The Kamikazes were symbolic of the fanaticism of the Japanese military in inflicting unavoidable death and injuries to our personnel, and extensive destruction to our craft. No one not directly exposed to the fury of the self-sacrificing Kamikazes could possibly imagine what would be in store for us if we undertook landings on the main island of Japan. Okinawa was a forerunner of what we could expect, if we were to venture a landing on the Japanese Islands.

While a large number of the Japanese civilian population as well as certain government officials had come to realize that defeat was imminent, (and that Japan had better come to terms with the United States), they were rendered impotent by the stranglehold the military held over the nation. Even the Emperor had no voice.

Although there had been a change in the cabinet, with Suzuki at its head, the military continued in absolute control. Suzuki privately advocated a peace settlement, but publicly he was for a war to the finish. His comment about the loss of Okinawa attested to his being under the military thumb when he dismissed the loss of Okinawa with "improved Japan's strategic position" and inflicted on America a "severe spiritual blow."

The entire Japanese economy was totally committed to war production. It was obvious that as long as military fanaticism was in control, there could be no reasoning with them. However, a newly installed cabinet had managed to send out some feelers to Russia to sound out possibilities for a peaceful settlement, but Russia was waiting in the wings to make a move that would serve the extension of her empire.

Almost from the day that Truman assumed the Presidency, Churchill had been pressing him for a joint meeting with Stalin. The death of President Roosevelt so soon after his Yalta meeting with Churchill and Stalin resulted in a serious breach in the plans to develop a working relationship with Russian participation in a peaceful world. The image of FDR as a leader of the free world symbolized the aspirations of mankind. Now that he was gone, the big question loomed large and perplexing: what manner of man was President Harry Truman, and are any of his policies going to differ in any significant way from that of his predecessor? This is what impelled Winston Churchill to press for a joint session at the earliest possible moment with President Truman and Stalin. It is fair to say that there were many questions in Stalin's own mind about the future that he was eager to resolve.

As for President Truman, he had many questions on his mind that required answers. One of these related to a Russian commitment to launch a second front against Japan in order to relieve some of the pressure on our own forces.

A meeting for Truman, Churchill and Stalin was finally agreed upon for July 17, 1945, at Potsdam. While Truman was en route, the American experimental bomb was set off at Alamagordo, New Mexico. Word of it was radioed to President Truman aboard ship.

Memorandum

~~Diff~~ I had not been
President very long
not more than a week
when Mr. Churchill
called me from London
and suggested a confer-
ence with Mr. Stalin
and himself. I told him
that I had to take over
the Presidency first and

over

53

Memorandum

that as soon as I had
things in line to leave
I would be glad to
meet with him and Italia.
These were the usual
troubles in the take over.
Although I had announc-
ed that I hoped President
Roosevelt's Cabinet would
stay with me, some of
them wanted to quit.
So these places had to

54

The Carlyle
35 EAST 76TH STREET
NEW YORK

Memorandum.

He pulled out, I had to send a policy message to the Congress and become adjusted to the Role of Decision Maker.

Mr. Churchill called me at least once a week and finally I told him I would meet with him and Stalin. But where would we meet? He

The Carlyle

35 EAST 76TH STREET
NEW YORK

Memorandum

Suggested some place in Germany. We agreed on Potsdam and the Prime Minister notified Stalin.

I arrived in Potsdam in due time and was put up in the Cecilia Hoff the former residence of the wife the Crown Prince of Germany.

A day or two later the

The Carlyle

35 EAST 76TH STREET
NEW YORK

Memorandum

Prime Minister came
in and then Mr. Stalin.
I arrived on the day set,
the other two were late.
Mr. Churchill paid his respects as soon as he ar-
rived, Stalin waited a day
and then came. They were
both very formal and very
pleasant.

I had prepared an ect-
jenda of the things I wanted

Memorandum

discussed. Neither Stalin
nor Churchill had any
set program. So I proceeded...

On his arrival at Potsdam, Truman shared with Churchill the news of this historic development—to Churchill's delight. In a somewhat veiled way, Truman hinted to Stalin that the United States had just achieved a great breakthrough in a totally new explosive. Stalin received the news with total impassivity.

Meanwhile, the Japanese military masters, driven by unabated fanaticism, were working feverishly for a long defensive siege. They regarded the mounting civilian casualties as expendable sacrifices. This disregard for human life, so characteristic of the Japanese military, was repugnant to the American people. It required very little imagination to see that if we were compelled to storm the Japanese shores and engage in combat with these Japanese fanatics, there would be incalculable casualties on both sides.

To avoid that kind of a carnage and as a way to end continued senseless destruction, Truman, Churchill and Chiang Kai-shek drafted an acceptable proposal for a prompt Japanese surrender. This became known as the Potsdam Declaration. These were the terms:

POTSDAM DECLARATION

1. The authority and influence of the Japanese militarists "must be eliminated for all time."

2. Until a "new order of peace, security and justice" in Japan, Allied forces will occupy Japanese key points "to secure the achievement" of this basic objective.

3. Terms of the Cairo Declaration will be carried out and Japanese sovereignty will be limited to Hokkaido, Honshuu, Kyushu, Shepoku and adjacent smaller islands.

4. Japanese military forces, after being completely disarmed, shall be permitted to return to their homes with the opportunity to lead peaceful and productive lives.

5. "We do not intend that the Japanese shall be enslaved as a race or destroyed as a nation, but stern justice shall be meted out to all war criminals...Freedom of speech, of religion, and of thought, as well as respect for the fundamental human rights, shall be established."

6. Japan may retain such industries as will sustain her economy, but not re-arm; and she may look forward to "participation in world trade relations."

7. Occupation forces "shall be withdrawn from Japan as soon as these objectives have been accomplished and there has been established a peacefully inclined and responsible government."

8. The Japanese government is called upon to "proclaim now the unconditional surrender of all Japanese armed forces." The alternative is "prompt and utter destruction."

On July 28th, Premier Suzuki announced at a press conference that the terms were unacceptable and rejected them out of hand, as had been the earlier Cairo Declaration. This action by Suzuki was at variance with the advice of his Foreign Minister Togo who counselled further consideration. But, his counsel was unavailing because Suzuki had slammed the door shut. This development was all the more distressing in light of Suzuki's follow-up statement that prospects for victory were improved because of increased aircraft production.

This foolhardy boast reinforced Truman's growing conviction that the Japanese military had resolved to exact a frightful price in American lives before they would consider surrender, notwithstanding the grim warning implicit in point #8 of the Potsdam Declaration. It had been talked about for some time that the Emperor on his own authority was taking steps to bring about an armistice. But, it was adroitly subverted by the ironclad military control.

The Potsdam meeting ended on the 13th day with yet no response from Tokyo. Truman boarded the USS Augusta to sail for home on August 2nd. In light of all the information transmitted to him together with the rejection of the Potsdam Declaration, there was no recourse but to make use of two atomic bombs to bring the war to a quick end. Truman continued to hope for some break in the Japanese position and was prepared to withdraw the order any moment.

However, the Japanese military continued to be indefeasible and oblivious to their inevitable defeat; they paid no heed to the efforts of their own Emperor and other voices of reason, and proceeded with their preparations for a determined stand to the very last.

The first bomb was dropped on Hiroshima on August 6th. It was inconceivable that the horrible, devastating power wrought by this bomb could have failed to restore the Japanese military to some measure of sanity. But again, they continued to act as if they didn't get the message— even as they could have averted the dropping of the next bomb.

After the second bomb was dropped on Nagasaki on August 9th, they were still clinging to a last ditch stand. Even at that point, the members of the Imperial Conference, ostensibly the highest authority in Japan, still persisted in impossible bargaining. They counterproposed such conditions as:

1. No military occupation of Japan.
2. No disarming of overseas troops.
3. No trial of war criminals by the Allies.

At the August 10th meeting of the Imperial Conference, the Emperor finally managed to assert his authority and indicated that he was willing to surrender Japan provisionally, on the basis of the terms outlined in the Potsdam Declaration. Even at this later point, the warlords were unable to reconcile to a defeat short of annihilation. They implored the Emperor to allow them to make one last effort to save the honor of Japan.

On August 14th, the Emperor's message was beamed around the world by Radio Tokyo that Japan had capitulated. The official notification of this decision was received by President Truman the same day. No news could have been more welcome to President Truman than having this terrible nightmare over with.

But, even after the Emperor had invoked his will for an immediate surrender (by recording a broadcast to be released the following day), the military hierarchy was plotting to sequester the recording and to seize the Emperor. Fortunately, that plot failed and the Emperor's message went out to the people.

Among the reasons postulated by the military to the Emperor for continued resistance (to which he was not persuaded) was that the atomic explosions were not very impressive, and that there was a reasonable chance that the enemy could be defeated by great kamikaze counterattacks. (They remained captives of their own elaborate power of self-delusion).

It was by adroit intervention of the Emperor that the kamikaze were kept grounded and frustrated in their planned attack on the USS Missouri as she was approaching to accept the surrender.

There was no mistaking the determination of the military even at the very end. Their fanatical zeal was sure to exact a frightful price of dead and wounded on both sides, had it been necessary to make a forced landing. There were over 5,000 kamikaze planes ready to be deployed, and there were one million trained soldiers ready for action on the home base. The loss of lives was calculated to be, at the least, 500,000 men on each side. The casualty figures and intelligence reports that reached Truman constantly kept emphasizing the nature of the opposition we yet had to face.

Lest we tend to forget, Russia had been invited to enter the war against Japan, and to open a second front in order to shorten the conflict. But she chose to wait. In the meantime, she had been dropping hints to the Japanese military that it was time to get rid of the Emperor. It was only after the first bomb was dropped on Hiroshima that Russia made haste to declare war on Japan. The obvious intent was to acquire a joint position with the United States in the occupation of Japan. This is how Russia brought about a division of Germany. Truman saw through that play and made sure that the United States would be solely in control.

The occupation of Japan was a classic example of how the conqueror becomes the benefactor. The United States inaugurated a program of reconstruction and restoration, and in short order helped to bring about an era of progress, prosperity and a democratic social order such as Japan had never known.

Following the use of an atomic bomb for the first time in the history of man, President Truman began to make plans for this instrument of war to become a means of keeping the peace of the world. At the time when we had sole custody and control of the atomic bomb, Truman recommended to the Congress and Congress voted its approval, that we turn over to the custody of the United Nations the possession and control of the production of nuclear weapons, and that we of the United States would at the same time destroy our own stockpile, and that, as a condition of this conveyance, a system of inspection be set up to make sure that there would be no cheating on the part of any nation. But, as a further condition, the United Nations was to assume responsibility not only for keeping the peace, but enforcing it as well. And, its sole possession of the atomic bomb would be used as its means for enforcing the peace.

Russia rejected inspection as a condition and went her own way in entering the Atomic Age, producing her own atomic stockpile. Her determination to enter in a contest with the United States forced other nations to join the Atomic Club.

But, inspite of this proliferation, let it be noted that since the Hiroshima/Nagaski "Demonstrations," no other instance of its use against man has occurred. There may be hope that fear may work where reason fails, and that the instinct for self preservation may yet prevail.

President Harry Truman receiving a special award as "The Outstanding Television Personality of 1964" from David Noyes, Producer of the TV series "Decisions...The Conflicts of Harry S. Truman."

Mr. Truman, David Noyes and Bill Hillman, while working together on the two-volume set of Memoirs

David Noyes with Rose Conway, long time personal secretary to Mr. Truman.

Mr. Truman in his White House office. The inscription reads: "To David Noyes, who helped me into slavery with satisfaction."

CHAPTER 6

1948 CAMPAIGN

In the Presidential campaign of 1948, the Democratic Party found itself facing a backlash reminiscent of the debacle it suffered in the 1920 post-war election. Truman was well aware of this, and many of his associates considered the outlook this time even more bleak. The Democratic Party had become fragmented. It was caught in political crosscurrents from the right, left, and even the middle. However, there was one big difference, and the difference was Truman. He never for a moment doubted that he would prevail.

In 1920, the Democrats nominated James M. Cox, a publisher from Ohio who had served with distinction as Governor of that state. The Republican Convention of 1920 found itself frozen in a deadlock. A small group in control of the convention retired into a room, (The original "smoke-filled room"), to compromise on a choice. They came up with Warren G. Harding, a United States Senator who, like Cox, was a publisher from Ohio. He projected the handsome exterior of an idealized president, but he had little else to recommend him.

The Democratic nominee was a far superior choice; he was worldly, articulate, highly educated, and a student of American history. In normal times, Cox, no doubt would have been swept into office. But, in the post-war atmosphere, Governor Cox was overwhelmingly rejected. He put up a valiant and energetic fight, travelling to every corner of the country, while

Harding confined his campaign to the front porch of his Marion, Ohio, home.

The strategist behind the Harding sweep was the dynamic and brilliant advertising man, Albert D. Lasker. He divined the political trend and mood of the people. They wanted a respite from the tensions and anxieties that had engulfed them in the war years. They wanted a breathing spell, and to Lasker with his ad-man acumen, all that spelled, "Let's get back to normalcy." And, that became the magic slogan. That kind of a campaign would not call for extensive travelling or barnstorming. Harding's front porch was a perfectly adequate platform for Lasker's siren song.

The morning following the landslide election of Harding, Governor Cox telephoned Lasker.

Cox:	"This is James Cox. Do you remember me?"
Lasker:	"How could I ever forget you?"
Cox:	"I was fully reconciled to a defeat, but I never thought that it would be so overwhelming. It occurred to me that the margin of my loss was in large measure due to your brilliant leadership of my opponent's campaign. I would like to salvage from this the privilege of your friendship. Where and when could we meet?"
Lasker:	"I have an appointment in Marion, Ohio, today to meet with Warren Harding, but that can wait. I can come to see you today instead."

Out of this exchange developed a lifelong friendship which was memorialized every year on Governor Cox's birthday. It was celebrated on Lasker's estate in Lake Forest, Illinois, where political and industrial leaders gathered to pay tribute to Cox. On these occasions, Governor Cox read one of his newly researched essays on early American history.

With Lasker close at hand, they became a well known foursome on the golf links: Harding. General Dawes, MacLean, and Lasker. To that extent, life in the Capitol was back to "normalcy" indeed.

Out of this tranquility, all hell was soon to break loose. Lasker had gained prior knowledge of an impending scandal of monumental corruption on the part of certain members of the Cabinet. It took an hour's briefing to unveil the whole plot to the President. Harding sat in stunned disbelief. Then, suddenly, he bolted out of his chair and turned on Lasker in livid anger. "Albert, I always regarded you as the most brilliant man I ever knew. Now I see you're stupid! How can you possibly think that men in such high and trusted positions could be so unpatriotic?"

Lasker abruptly took his leave, packed up his belongings, and left Washington. It wasn't long before the dam burst. The President was shocked and bewildered. All the ugly aspects of the Teapot Dome Scandal descended upon him. He found himself implicated in a national tragedy that he couldn't bear and wouldn't survive.

In 1948, after a long period of political subordination, the Republicans were now preparing for the takeover. Their optimism had its roots in their 1946 election victories, when they took control of both the House and the Senate.

Dewey had good reason to be confident, smug and self-satisfied. Wallace attracted to himself some segments of the liberals and the Leftists. Strom Thurmond launched a secessionist movement to sever the solid south from the Democratic Party. To Dewey, all of these added up to an almost impossible hurdle for the President to negotiate.

The disorientation of the Democrats was well demonstrated on the convention floor in Chicago. There were many angry voices in defiance of Truman. There were those whose announced candidacies were calculated to block the nomination of HST. The Dixiecrats, who never forgave Truman for this advocacy of civil rights, raised their strident voices and ultimately walked out of the convention.

Throughout all the clamor and oratory, Truman, alone in his room, waited for the convention to settle down; he was confident that, in the end, the convention would endorse him. When his nomination seemed certain, he was summoned to deliver his speech of acceptance. However, as he reached the hall, there were still some diehards who insisted on being heard. It was already late, but HST was forced to wait out these last few zealous orators from the confines of a small room above the railroad tracks. (He understood that this kind of seemingly discordant behavior was not unusual in a free and open convention.) It was not until nearly 2:00 a.m. that he finally received word of his nomination.

When at last Truman appeared, the exhausted and wilted delegates came to life. They greeted him with an uproarious standing ovation. HST responded with a rousing, challenging speech. His first lines were, "Senator Bradley and I will win this election and make these Republicans like it. Don't you forget that!" He threw down the gauntlet to the opposition; he dared the Congress to make good on its responsibilities to the "Common everyday man." The delegates were electrified and rose to their feet in sustained acclaim. This was the portentous beginning of what turned out to be one of the most historic upsets in this nation's history.

Truman knew he had a monumental struggle ahead of him, and that he had to plan his campaign strategy very adroitly. He invited me to work with him as a personal advisor. We met privately from time to time, either in the Oval Room or in his living quarters, and conferred about the strategy. In my private sessions with him, when we discussed various approaches to his strategy, he would keep asserting that he was bound to win. I asked him once whether his confidence in the outcome was based on some precedent in history, or some special insight he had that was obviously denied to the rest of us. He said, "I base it on something fundamental; that is, a knowledge of the people, for people never knowingly vote against themselves. Once they are given to understand what it is they are to vote for or against, they will know what to do. And, as the campaign gets going, I intend to hammer the issues home. The people are a great deal smarter than some credit them with. Once they are convinced that they can trust you, the outcome is assured."

In the course of the campaign, Henry Wallace was beginning to make perceptible headway by attracting to himself a sizeable following, lured to that battle cry of "peace at any price." Truman had a special liking for Wallace. He regarded him as the ablest Secretary of Agriculture in the nation's history. (He had served eight years in that capacity under President Roosevelt.) His creation of hybrid corn was a great contribution to society. But, with all that, he was a mystic and intellectually suggestible.

As a matter of historic fact, the peace issue was misappropriated by Wallace and promulgated under false pretenses. The Truman commitment to the peace of the world was total and all embracing. The usurpation of this theme by Wallace's visionary preachments had to be countermanded by a more practical approach.

In 1945, after Roosevelt appointed Wallace to the post of Secretary of Commerce, (Vice President Truman's tie-breaking vote made the confirmation), he took to the road with missionary zeal in preachments on the peace theme and in criticism of the U. S. foreign policy. When Truman became President a few months later, Wallace increased his criticism of American policy at the expense of his post as Secretary of Commerce. Through the months he made numerous foreign policy speeches, at home as well as on foreign platforms, without clearing them with Truman. Much as the President liked Wallace, he could no longer tolerate such insubordination and presumption. Thereupon, on September 20, 1945, the President dispatched a note to Wallace which read: "Upon receipt of this letter, you will no longer be Secretary of Commerce."

Wallace picked up the phone and asked to speak to the President. He was put through at once. He said, addressing the President by his first name, "Harry, I've just received your letter. I'm sending it back. Please send me a nice one." Truman did. Despite this unhappy encounter, their friendship remained unbroken through the years.

In his campaign for the Presidency, Wallace continued to hammer away on his one theme: the peace issue. In the wake of the recent war, this was a timely and appealing issue. The polls were beginning to reflect this incursion which the Truman campaign could ill afford.

Despite the long hours that Truman put into his campaign, he kept a steady eye on developments in the foreign field. About this time, Russia was beginning to flex her muscles with a tendency to go it alone, especially in the ominous expansion of nuclear development. There was desperate need for close cooperation in this field. Our representatives were received coldly and distantly. We were simply unable to communicate, and there was no way that we could see that a breakthrough was likely to occur. Secretary Marshall was having sensitive meetings with foreign secretaries in Paris to see what could be done about lessening world tensions. Wallace was skillfully capitalizing on this issue.

What President Truman was anxiously searching for was a breakthrough to the developing intransigence of Russian hierarchy. All approaches thus far had proved futile. A comparable situation occurred immediately after the First World War. Through a series of misunderstandings and misjudgments, there developed a serious strain in the relations of the United States and Great Britain. Efforts at reconciliation by high level government representatives on both sides proved unavailing. The situation was deadlocked.

Then, Great Britain came up with a brilliant stroke by deciding to approach the problem on a non-governmental level. Lord Chief Justice Reading, clearly a man above the crowd in all respects, was enlisted to undertake such a mission. (He was uninvolved in party politics or the government establishment).

Lord Reading came to Washington and quietly arranged a series of meetings with key people in the government. All conversations were private. There were no speeches and no press conferences. It was all casual, quiet and informal. The personal credibility, quiet reasoning, and the judicial approach on the part of Lord Reading made it work. He went as quietly as he came, leaving behind him an enduring impression of a highly skillful performance that will long be remembered.

It occurred to us that we might undertake a similar mission to Russia with our own Chief Justice Vinson whose position and character also were above partisan politics and above the crowd. The President reacted enthusiastically to the idea, and he immediately summoned Vinson.

When they met, the President took up the troublesome matter of our inability to achieve some accommodation with the Russians in our plans for world peace. The President then reminded Vinson how, at another time in recent history, England had called upon its Chief Justice, Lord Reading, to undertake such a high level mission in the interest of restoring peaceful detente, the outcome of which proved to be one of the bright chapters in the annals of international relations.

"Now," he said to Vinson, "I wish you would consider a similar undertaking on behalf of this nation. We are unable to negotiate with Russia on a cooperative basis. They are beset with suspicion and mistrust."

At first, Chief Justice Vinson demurred, asserting that he did not think that this would be a proper function for a member of the Court. "But then," he added, "I will do it, if you order me to."

And the President said, "In that case, I'm asking you to go."

On the eve of Vinson's departure, the President planned to make a major foreign policy statement on the networks to explain the meaning and the purpose of the Vinson mission. But, a leak (ascribed to someone in the State Department) to a Washington correspondent for the *Chicago Tribune*, disclosed the mission prematurely, causing an angry protest from Marshall.

Marshall, who was then in Paris, was having sensitive meetings with foreign ministers on ways to overcome the mounting difficulties between East and West. He immediately telephoned the President and served notice that if Truman insisted on going through with the Vinson mission, Marshall would have no choice but to tender his resignation. He felt that his work would be seriously handicapped and his standing compromised.

The President was badly shaken by this development. For the first time, these two men had run into a crisis of friendship. The President found himself facing a perplexing dilemma. On the one hand, he had set his heart and high hopes on a mission that could have opened the doors to a better understanding with the Kremlin. On the other hand, he was not prepared to pay the price of a split with Marshall. He cancelled the mission forthwith.

Having done that, he called me into his office, and after a painful pause, said, "Dave, I've let you down, and I will understand if you tell me off." This was Harry Truman in his most appealing posture. He knew that we had worked hard and long hours in the research and drafting of his statement. He knew that we, as he, had high expectations on the outcome of the Vinson mission, and that we had to be deeply disappointed. But, we also understood how deeply disappointed he was on his own account.

My response was the only one I had in me to make. "Mr. President, you did what you thought you had to do. I have always respected your motives and never ascribed to them any measure of weakness on your part." We all went back to work.

The President suggested that perhaps we could salvage something out of the aborted mission by using part of his prepared statement during his scheduled appearance before the American Legion Convention at Miami on October 19th. This was precisely the kind of audience he wanted to address on the subject of peace. (It was a subject unlike any that a President was expected to make to a convention of veterans.)

Truman addressed the veterans in his usual direct, unembellished style. "...In recently considering sending a special emissary to Moscow, my purpose was to ask Premier Stalin's cooperation in dispelling the present poisonous atmosphere of distrust which now surrounds the negotiations between the Western Powers and the Soviet Union. My emissary was to convey the seriousness and sincerity of the people of the United States in their desire for peace."

"This proposal had no relation to existing negotiations within the scope of the United Nations or the Council of Foreign Ministers...The purpose of this mission was to improve the atmosphere in which they must take place and help in producing fruitful and peaceful results..."

It was evident that the veterans had been reached. Instead of the usual catcalls, President Truman received a standing ovation. They listened, and they believed him.

In an important way, this speech served to revitalize and regenerate the public understanding of the President's total commitment to world peace, and thus may have slowed the Wallace drive for the Presidency.

In the prevailing climate, it was inevitable that the 1948 campaign would get off to a slow, faltering start amidst predictions of inevitable defeat. This was the feeling that permeated members of the staff and the cabinet, some of whom were already engaged in considering other opportunities. That, however, was not the mood of Truman. He was steadfast in his conviction that he would prevail. Truman kept up a steady drive to get his programs across to the people. He kept hammering away on the theme of the 'Gluttons of Privilege' and the failings of the "do-nothing" 80th Congress. But, a sizeable segment continued to favor Wallace; the South, of course, had to be written off. Dewey, with the polls showing him far ahead, was basking in the comfort of his ineluctability.

Truman, on occasion, would depart from his forthright style and cut loose with a few humorous barbs aimed at his opponent's vulnerability. When the polls continued to reaffirm the trend toward Dewey, Truman responded with, "The Republicans take a poll and go to sleep!" At times he would resort to a bit of mockery; he would quote selected passages from Dewey's speeches, all the while twisting an imaginary mustache.

Week after week, the pollsters kept repeating themselves. It was like a broken record. One of them, the highly regarded, scholarly Elmo Roper, threw in the towel. His findings were published in the *New York Herald Tribune*. Some considerable time before the election, he terminated his analysis of the campaign with the declaration that the outcome was so obviously certain that further polls would be redundant.

Elmo Roper was a close and valued friend of mine. (We visited from time to time, and oftener when he became president of The Fund for the Republic at Santa Barbara.) In our visits after the election, I had refrained from bringing up his miscalculation. I wanted to spare him the embarrassment. But, one day at lunch, I finally put the question to him. How could he, of all people, have been so unaware of the trend that was beginning to develop for Truman? His answer was one for the books. "I can't really account for it, especially in the light of the fact that all members of my family and I voted for Harry Truman."

As the campaign was drawing to a close, I accompanied the President on the last train ride that he would make before winding up at Independence. I noted that through the farming areas and in the steel towns of Gary, Hammond, etc., in Indiana, great numbers of people met the train, showering their goodwill upon the President. To me, it looked as though the campaign had at last achieved a breakthrough, and prospects for victory were looking more hopeful.

We arrived at the Chicago 12th Street Station early Friday morning. I joined the President and Mrs. Truman on the back platform of the train to bid them farewell; I would be returning to Los Angeles that afternoon. As I shook hands with the President, he gave me an affectionate hug and said…

"You were with me all the way in this campaign and I shall never forget it. Without your guidance and direction I don't think we would have made it."

"You made the difference."

THE WHITE HOUSE
WASHINGTON

November 13, 1948

Dear Dave:

You were very kind indeed to send me such a nice message at Kansas City, and I am more grateful to you than I can say for all that you did to assure a successful outcome of the campaign.

I was confident that if the American people knew the facts, we could rely on their good judgment. It was the loyal assistance of good friends like yourself that made it possible to present all the facts to them.

Very sincerely yours,

Harry Truman

Mr. David Noyes,
1-901 Levering Avenue,
Los Angeles 24,
California.

CHAPTER 7

FEDERAL RESERVE

Throughout his public career, Truman exhibited a keen interest in fiscal matters. As President, he regarded the budget as one of the highest priorities among the major responsibilities of his office. He was the first president to initiate the presentation of the budget at a press conference. Employing a blackboard and pointer, he explained before TV cameras the key items in the budget and how they were arrived at before being submitted to the Congress for its approval.

An anomaly to the three branches of government was the Federal Reserve Board. It evolved into a fourth branch of the government, but not a coordinate branch. Because of its unique position in the system of governmental operations, where it was not beholden either to the executive or the legislative, it occasionally embarked on ventures and decisions which did not coincide with the national interest. As it was originally set up, it was to be a totally autonomous branch of the government, neither responsible nor accountable to anyone in the government for any of its decisions.

The original intent was to prevent political consideration on the part of either the Congress or the Executive Branch from intruding on Federal Reserve procedures. However, President Truman had come to feel that the Federal Reserve was no longer functioning primarily for the purpose for which it was established.

Throughout most of its history, the government of the United States has had to deal with fiscal problems. As the nation grew, these problems became more complex. President Andrew Jackson, (one of Truman's heroes), who instituted many reforms, considered establishing a Bank of the United States in order to take the management of federal financing out of the control of private banking institutions. However, it was not until the Presidency of Woodrow Wilson that monetary control of the nation was delegated to an independent government agency. It required an act of Congress to empower it with the authority to exercise autonomous control over its decisions and regulations. Senator Carter Glass, who in his own right was an expert in the field of fiscal policies, piloted the legislation through the Senate. Shortly after its enactment, he became the first Secretary of the Treasury to work within the new system.

The members of the "Fed"—seven in all—were to be appointed by the president for a term of fourteen years. The Chairman of the "Fed" was to be appointed by the President as well. Having made the appointments, the President's authority ceased. This vested in the Federal Reserve Board enormous power which it was supposed to use with diligence and circumspection, and with due regard for the fiscal needs of the nation. Regrettably, the "Fed" had strayed from time to time from its assigned purpose, resulting in difficult periods for this nation.

HST maintained a constant vigil over the government's fiscal condition. In his cabinet, John Snyder, Secretary of the Treasury, a lifelong friend and a successful conservative banker, worked hand in glove with him in surveillance.

Truman worked closely with the Bureau of the Budget in an effort to arrive at a balanced budget. In the immediate post-war period, he was able to manage it, but he was gaining on it. His goal was, not only to balance the budget, but to start paying off the national debt. Then it happened. In the years of 1947, 1948, and 1951, HST presented to the nation not only a balanced budget, but a substantial surplus as well. From that time on, HST expected to show a surplus each year. However, the Korean affair subverted that hope.

The Korean involvement was a new source of drain on the Treasury. In a move of the worst possible timing, the Federal Reserve Board, at its meeting, voted on three directives that would impose needless burdens on the government's ability to finance its operations. The Federal Reserve informed the Secretary of the Treasury of its actions at its regular meeting, and these were as follows:

1. The rediscount rate to banks is to be substantially higher.
2. The interest rate on Treasury borrowing is to be increased.
3. The Federal Reserve will no longer take up any unsubscribed portion of federal issues.

Secretary of Treasury John Snyder reported to the President this arbitrary and untimely action by the governors of the Federal Reserve. The President invited the Board to meet with him with a view to having this action rescinded. The meeting ended on a note of conciliation and a commitment from the Board to postpone indefinitely its decisions. For reasons best known to itself, the Board decided to back on its commitment to the President and held to its original three-point program.

Secretary Snyder immediately rushed over to report the bad news to the President. The President told Secretary Snyder to get in touch with the Chairman of the Federal Reserve Board to ask him to come to see the President the next morning. On his arrival, the Chairman was reminded by the President of the unfortunate timing of its decisions as they would obviously impose a serious hardship on the government at a very difficult period. Moreover, he pointed out that the government was already saddled with an enormous interest burden which was reflected in the taxes to our citizens.

The Chairman regretted to inform the President that the deed was done, that it constituted the unanimous action by the Board, and that there was no way to undo it.

The President challenged the finality of that position. Said he, "Need I remind you that the final authority in this nation is derived from the people? Since your decision is against the public interest, I cannot accept it as final. There are some options open to me that I intend to put to use. One of these is to go before a Joint Session of the Congress and ask for a revision of the Board's charter; (that, however, might prove to be too drastic). Another option would be to go on the networks and lay the problem directly before the American people. But there is a simpler alternative. Why don't you resign?"

The Chairman reacted, "Are you asking me to resign, Mr. President?"

"No, I'm not. You know that once you are appointed, I do not have the authority to dismiss you. It is only a suggestion."

To that the Chairman responded, "When would you want me to resign?"

"Would tomorrow morning be too soon?" answered the President.

The Chairman appeared the next morning and tendered his resignation. The President then called in William McChesney Martin, Undersecretary of the Treasury. On his arrival, HST said to him, "Bill, I intend to appoint you as the new chairman of the Federal Reserve Board, but after I appoint you, I will not have any authority over you. Therefore, I have to exact a promise from you beforehand—that the recent actions taken by the Board will be rescinded, and I want that as a commitment."

They shook hands on it, and when Martin took over as Chairman of the Board, all of these troublesome decisions were removed. And, that's the way it stayed throughout the remainder of President Truman's term.

In 1966, when LBJ was in the White House, at a time when we were overextended in our Vietnam commitment, the Federal Reserve moved inopportunely once again by raising the discount rate. Truman regarded that as a very unwise move and felt that it would set into play an inflationary spiral and sow the seeds of economic depression. He was so deeply alarmed that he decided to issue a public statement on the subject. An abbreviated press version is reproduced herewith.

Truman warns of depression

KANSAS CITY, Mo. (UPI) — Former President Harry S. Truman said Sunday a "drastic increase in interest rates has been imposed on the American economy" and warned that higher rates could result in "a serious depression."

Truman, in a strongly worded prepared statement, called the rising interest rates "a matter about which I am so deeply concerned that I feel it has become necessary for me to speak out."

David Noyes, a longtime Truman associate, distributed the statement. He said Truman had worked on it for the past three days because he was "bothered" by the upward climb of interest rates.

"I rarely, these days, take up pen to make comment on matters which I am confident are receiving the concern and attention of the administration," the statement said.

"But, I thought that this was a matter which had reached the point where it became necessary for me to speak. There is yet time to remedy the situation," the statement said.

The 81-year-old Truman, who left office in January, 1953, said "a warning is current that higher rates are yet to come.

"Of course, no one wants run away inflation. But, I think it is fair to say that that kind of inflation is no longer possible in the United States.

"What is more likely to happen is that we will bring on a precipitous deflation, if we persist in high interest practices. The result could be a serious depression," the statement said.

Aug. 28 — 1966

91

Truman's interest and skill in dealing with fiscal problems and his understanding of them goes back to the days when he was presiding judge of Jackson County. While in that office, he instituted a program of building a network of highways connecting the rural areas with the center of Kansas City. It involved a bond issue of considerable size, running in excess of $30 million, and at a time when the affairs of the nation, particularly the money market, were in a depressed state.

He made a trip to Chicago to call on a group of bankers on LaSalle Street to whom he submitted a carefully detailed projection of the contemplated project and how the repayments were to be met. The underwriters were interested, but they figured that they would have to impose a rate of interest at 4 1/2% or possibly 4 3/4 %. It was a higher figure than Truman felt they were justified in charging. He argued, "Look. We are a very sound operation; we pay our bills; the fiscal policies of Jackson County rate high. What's more, these are tax anticipation warrants, and they deserve the lowest prevailing rate. The County's record is one of the best in the country. I came here prepared to negotiate a rate somewhere around 3 1/2% and that is all you ought to charge for such a sound issue."

The underwriters were adamant and insisted on the higher rate. Then, Truman rose to leave. "Well, if that's the way you all feel about it, I guess I have to go to New York where I'm sure I can get a more favorable rate of interest."

This brought the underwriters up sharply, and they asked for time to reconsider. They retired into a closed session and soon filed back to inform Judge Truman that they would meet his terms.

CHAPTER 8

STATE OF ISRAEL

One of the many historic decisions Harry Truman was to make was that of the establishment of the State of Israel. It was not his most difficult decision, but it was a trying one. His erudition in the realm of history and indeed, his mastery of the Bible, equipped him with an understanding of that ancient world. He had a vision for the rebirth of that part of the world. The realization of it depended upon the establishment of a State of Israel where industry would flourish and thus stimulate the development and prosperity of all the nations in that part of the world.

Truman was prepared to face up to the negative postures of many key members in his administration, leaders in the Congress, and especially that of his own Secretary of State. He could never brush aside or erase from his memory the horrible atrocities perpetrated by the Nazis against these people, or dismiss it as a bygone human catastrophe. Moreover, constitutionally, the responsibility was his to interpret the traditional foreign policy of the United States and its concern for the plight of humanity.

An exchange of letters in 1956 with Mrs. Eleanor Roosevelt attests to Truman's unflagging interest in that part of the world. HST's letter follows:

January 19, 1956

Dear Dave:

The purpose of this note is to ask for Anna Roosevelt's correct name and address. I want to send her my edition of the memoirs, but ' don't know where she's living now.

I have enclosed a copy of a letter I wrote yesterday to her mother. I thought it might interest you.

The trip to Minnesota was a very successful one. The attendance at the dinner Saturday night was rounded out by about four hundred farmers who paid a hog each for their tickets. Twenty-five dollars cash is mighty hard for them to come by these days.

Sincerely yours,

Harry Truman

Hon. David M. Noyes
9489 Dayton Way
Beverly Hills, California

January 18, 1956

Dear Mrs. Roosevelt:

I was very pleased to receive your letter of the
thirteenth enclosing the suggested statement on the
Near East, and I am in complete accord with your view
that something must be done.

While I was President of the United States, I had
a survey made of the whole Near East. Gordon Clapp went
to the Valley of the Tigris and the Euphrates and came
back with the report that it is perfectly feasible to
restore those old canals constructed and used by the
ancient Babylonians and the people of Ninevah under Sen-
nacherib. With that irrigation the land could support
from twenty to thirty million people. He said that
there are 160 billion barrels of oil in sight in the
Arabian desert and also that it is quite possible to run
a syphon from the Mediterranean to the Dead Sea Valley
which would create enough power to make Israel a completely industrial nation.

Dr. Bennett of Oklahoma A. & M., who worked with
me on the Point IV program, spent the previous year in
Ethiopia where he found a plateau of about 62,000 square
miles at from six to eight thousand feet above sea level
where the soil is as rich and black as it is in the Iowa
corn belt. His estimate was that it could raise enough
food for a hundred million people.

As you know, we succeeded in getting Turkey to
raise a surplus of food stuffs. The last year I was in
the White House that country raised a surplus of four
million tons of wheat. Before that, it had had to im-
port wheat from Russia.

That shows what proper development could do for the whole area, from the Adriatic Sea right around the Mediterranean to Libya, and Israel would be its industrial center.

The Nile River is being developed now, and eventually the Egyptians, who haven't had enough to eat since the first Pharaoh, will be able to feed another twenty million people.

I hope you will forgive me for taking up your time with this long dissertation, but I am extremely interested in that part of the world.

Whenever you are ready, send me the document, and I will be very happy to sign it.

Sincerely yours,

HARRY S. TRUMAN

Mrs. Franklin D. Roosevelt
211 East 62nd Street
New York 21, N. Y.

As the President was deeply involved in effectuating his decision, he found himself beset and besieged with many pressures and crosscurrents of opinion that impinged on his time and tried his patience. A steady stream of well wishers and self-appointed advisors pressed for audiences with him, but he could only accommodate a few. But even that proved to be a mistake. To put an end to these self-appointed spokesmen, he issued an order to his Appointment Secretary, Matthew J. Connelly, that there would be no more appointments on the question, and that there were to be no exceptions. This edict caused a wave of alarm among leaders of the Jewish community who insisted they had a right to be heard.

Against this background, it was announced that Dr. Weitzman was arriving in the United States. Truman knew and respected Dr. Weitzman, not only as a great scientist but as a statesman, but the order barring appointments would prevent Dr. Weitzman from paying his respects to President Truman. Dr. Weitzman was the symbol and hope for the eventual re-establishment of the State of Israel. To the American Jewish constituency, it was unthinkable that the President would refuse to see him. In desperation appeals for help began to flood in on Eddie Jacobson.

Eddie Jacobson occupied a special place in the life of Harry Truman. It began when they both served in France during the First World War, and they remained fast friends ever since. As Truman moved up the political ladder from County Judge to the Presidency, his devotion to his little Sergeant never waivered. Whenever HST came home to look in on his mother, the Secret Service men were instructed to stop at Eddie's store first. He would always greet Jacobson with the usual, "How's business, Eddie?"

The answer invariably would be, "Getting better all the time, Mr. President." (From the moment HST because President, Eddie no longer used the familiar "Harry." He could not bring himself to overcome his awe of the Presidency.) He was determined to stay out of the public eye and kept his relationship totally private.

Eddie was offered all manner of deals and propositions, some involving large investments, in which he stood to profit greatly, if he would arrange the right contacts in government, all of which he categorically rejected out of hand. Under no circumstances would he capitalize on his friendship with the President.

However, events conspired to propel Eddie Jacobson into a new role. A stream of calls from every part of the country poured in on him, beseeching him to see the President and to plead with him to receive Dr. Weitzman. Suddenly Eddie became a man possessed, and as he put it, "My people are calling me for help. I must go."

Eddie flew to Washington, registered at the Statler Hotel, and immediately called Matt Connelly for an appointment to see the President. Matt responded warmly with, "Hello, Eddie, for you there is no need for an appointment. We have standing instructions from the President that whenever you are here, you are to come right over. So, come ahead."

After some hesitation, Eddie said, "But, Matt, this is not personal. I have come to see him about Dr. Weitzman."

"In that case, Eddie," said Connelly, "I had better ask him first." When he returned to the phone, he said, "The President said for you to come right over, but that under no circumstances must you discuss Dr. Weitzman with him."

Eddie replied, "I will just have to take my chances." Matt Connelly so reported it to the President.

Eddie had but a short wait, and then, as he was ushered into the President's office, he found that for the first time in their long friendship, the President received him very distantly. He did not shake hands with him, nor did he ask him to sit down. The President walked over to the window looking out on the Rose Garden, turning his back on Eddie. In a bewildered state, Eddie sat down. After an awkward moment, he erupted into an emotional outburst. Pounding the desk with his fist, he shouted, "God dammit, Harry! You've got to see him! He's the George Washington of my people!" In his plight, he seemed to have lost control of his sense in addressing the President by his first name. A different Eddie Jacobson suddenly emerged.

Still, there was no response from the President. Eddie pounded the table again. He began to plead, "But Harry, do you remember when we were in the store together? You sat on the balcony reading about George Washington while I attended to the business downstairs. We got along very well, didn't we, in those days? Well, Dr. Weitzman is the George Washington of my people. Won't you please make an exception and see him?"

"Why," interjected the President, smiling at Eddie, "You little bald-headed so-and-so!" All at once Eddie realized that all was well again as in the days of yore. Walking back to the desk, the President said, "Of course, I'll see him, Eddie, but I'll see him only for you. You see, Eddie, there's really no need for me to see Dr. Weitzman because he and I have a clear understanding. He knows where I stand. But, I will see him on one condition and that is that you accompany him through the side door, and we have our visit off the record.

While I was working on the "Memoirs," Eddie Jacobson came to the office and said he had something to put into the record and wanted to talk to me privately. The foregoing is based on that interview.

On the occasion of the Eddie Jacobson Memorial President Truman made the following comments:

"...I don't think I have ever known a man that I thought more of outside of my own family than I did of Eddie Jacobson. He was an honorable and as I said in my Memoirs, that I published here not long ago, he was one of the finest men that ever walked this earth, and that's covering a lot of territory in my knowledge of people that I have seen, and I think I have come in contact with about as many people as any one man ever did. Eddie was one of those men that you read about in the Torah, and I have a Torah that the President of Israel gave me that's one of the greatest things I own, and he issued an injunction as President of Israel, authorizing a Baptist to handle it. And I am of the opinion that if you read the articles in Genesis concerning just two men-one of them was Enoch and the other Noah—you'll find those descriptions fit Eddie Jacobson to the dot. So, when you honor Eddie Jacobson, you honor me, and I thank you for it. And I leave you with one thought, that the State of Israel will find stability and progress, and from

Isaiah, 'They shall beat their swords into plow shares, and their spears into pruning-hooks; nation shall not lift up sword against nation, neither shall they learn war any more.' This is my prayer for peace. I thank you."

There were two primary objectives in HST's approach to the problem of Israel. Uppermost was the humanitarian concern. He felt that what had happened in Germany was a blot on the civilized world, and he would see to it that that act of savagery would never be relegated to the archives of history. Perhaps, had the Balfour Declaration been implemented in its day, that frightful carnage might not have occurred. At long last, he reasoned, there was an obvious way for civilized peoples to provide, in partial atonement, a homeland for those persecuted and long abused people.

The other objective had to do with the revitalization of that historic part of the world where civilization took root. This was a life-long dream of his and vision of the future.

In a historic sense, he held a high hope for the evolution of that entire part of the world. He saw that the State of Israel could hasten that rebirth. He felt that with their capacity for inventiveness, industry and commerce, it could have major influence on the developments of the other nations surrounding it and to the betterment of all its people. He hoped there would be a kind of a Renaissance as in the days of the Garden of Eden. By harnessing the Euphrates and the Nile, and by the desalinization of sea water, a great agricultural development could blossom in that area. Equally important to that end was the restoration of impoverished land through massive application of fertilizers derived from petroleum sources so abundant in the region.

Truman's vision for that part of the world went even beyond the Middle East areas. He felt living conditions in much of Africa could be advanced by introducing the means and skills of a revitalized Middle East into that part of the world. Truman always associated the establishment of the State of Israel as an indispensable stimulant for a revitalized flourishing Middle East.

The following address was delivered by Former President of the United States Harry S. Truman, at the United Jewish Appeal Luncheon, at the Waldorf-Astoria Hotel in New York City on May 11, 1964.

"I have been having a wonderful time these days with my friends, who with each passing year, seem more determined to make something of my birthday. I have tried to discourage them from reminding me of my birthday-but they would not hear of it-so I keep giving in to them, because I did not want to disappoint them-and, frankly, I enjoy every minute of it!

Reaching eighty is considered to be some kind of a landmark for any mortal, especially for one who happened to have survived the rigors of the White House test of endurance.

I have been looking forward to being with you today, not only because I wanted to do what I could to help the good cause of the annual United Jewish Appeal, but I also had some things on my mind, and in my heart, that I wanted to tell you about.

This nation is presently engaged in a <u>reaffirmation</u> and a <u>debate</u> on how, at long last, we are to make good on our constitutional commitment that none of our citizens be deprived of his or her civil rights in any state in the Union.

This unfinished business has been upsetting us <u>internally</u> and hurting us <u>externally</u>. We have let it divert us from many constructive measures we must take to meet the growing needs of our population. This condition has been going on long enough-too long in fact! So, I say, let us settle this debt to this large group of our neglected citizens, once and for all and be done with it!

We must all realize that there is no longer any valid reason to keep putting off a decision made a hundred years ago-that all human beings are entitled to equal treatment. And that freedom is not something to be rationed on the basis of race or religion.

Today, I regret to say, there are still those among us who would like to see the settlement deferred for another hundred years, if, indeed, not forever. This is a die-hard position-and they know it won't work, but they won't stop trying-not even after we put the pending legislation on the books.

They give us all sorts of arguments in their opposition to any civil rights legislation that we cannot legislate tolerance into human nature, or that we cannot go against human nature, or that we cannot force people to accept people they don't like. And that we had best leave the matter to the states to do as they think best.

These people confuse their public obligation with their private social rights. The one is a duty-the other a privilege. An organized free society cannot leave the choice of public conduct to the will and whim of the individual.

We have to have rules of conduct and the laws to enforce them.

To defer to the discretion of the individual, or to any one or more states in such critical areas as civil rights, is to invite trouble.

So much for the current conflict in our society.

Today, I would also like to call attention to another form of discrimination that has been troubling me for many, many years: how to overcome the bad habit of discrimination and persecution of the Jewish people in so many places. These people, our friends and good neighbors, are still being victimized in this twentieth century-we like to call it the century of liberation.

But where are those voices of strong protest against denial of equal rights to our Negro population, or the practice of another kind of discrimination-we know as anti-Semitism? Why do we not hear them now?

Where were these people all the time that discrimination and exclusion were practiced against our Jewish citizens in so many insidious ways?

We seem to have little trouble in forgiving those who make war on us and perpetrate ravages and destruction against us. Yet some carry a permanent grudge against the Jewish people. I find that hard to understand.

We did not hesitate to go to the aid of Germany after a terrible war, and in spite of the horrors they perpetuated. We did it because we thought that it was the right thing to do-and events proved it was.

Why is it that after the attack on us at Pearl Harbor, which President Franklin Roosevelt denounced before Congress as an act of treachery that would long live in infamy, that we nevertheless extended a helping hand to the Japanese people-fallen enemy?

We, moreover, contributed much of our wealth to restore Japan, so it could take an honorable and constructive place among the free nations of the world. We adopted this humane course because it was the right thing to do and also because of the developing world situation.

Time has proved that our effort to establish friendly relations with post war Japan was of significant help to the West.

What other people had been so cruelly mistreated as the Jews in the persecution they suffered in Czarist Russia, Nazi Germany, the Spanish Inquisition-and elsewhere to the days of the Pharaohs?

With the Communists now in control of Russia, what about the situation of the Jews there now? The Communists keep telling the world in their propaganda how, under the "new order" there would no longer be any barriers or discrimination against any race or nationality-and that henceforth the entire population would receive equal treatment.

But, we all know that it is not exactly the case. There is as much persecution of Jews in Soviet Russia now as there was in the days of Czarist Russia.

This historic saga of persecution is one of the reasons why, as President, I placed a high priority on the establishment of the new State of Israel. I hoped that by this action the people of the United States would help to right a terrible wrong. For I deeply felt that the persecution of Jews over the centuries has left a deep and ugly scar on the conscience of civilization.

Anti-Semitism is not a trait anyone is born with. It is something akin to a communicable disease-passed on from community to parent, and from parent to child. And the cycle goes on generation after generation.

The disease of anti-Semitism is so virulent that each generation seems to be helplessly caught up in it. And there is no effective cure in sight, save that of an awakened conscience of man. What I find even more discouraging is to see that in our institutions of higher education, where one would expect the intellectual ferment to act as a purifier, there, too, prejudice, discrimination and exclusion exist in one guise or another.

And we know that in some of our large *business* institutions, as in our professions of law, medicine and other fields, discrimination and exclusion are not uncommon.

What I am saying here is not intended to minimize the seriousness of the problem of the Negro in the United States. This, most of us have long recognized, and know that we must correct.

But I do think it is about time that we face up to the offensive treatment *accorded* Jewish people here and elsewhere. And it is about time someone said something about the violation of not only their <u>civil rights</u> but in certain areas their very lives *as we* consider how the tiny State of Israel, only a few years along from its precarious beginning, has had to live with neighboring nations, who are fanatically resolved to destroy it by every means.

And what about our churches-what have they done? Here, too, our spiritual leaders have proved ineffectual-and the persecution of this mere handful of people scattered throughout the four corners of the world-goes on unabated. Even at the Vatican, where historic reforms are under consideration, the problem of anti-Semitism had to be tabled for lack of agreement.

And, so I say, the issue of civil rights is with us in many manifestations. The plight of the Negroes is but one of these. Anti-Semitism is as grave a challenge to our sense of fairness and morality. It is to the everlasting credit of the Jewish people that they have managed to live with all their troubles and to survive them.

When I think of the question of civil rights in full perspective, I am moved to say as the Lord said in Green Pastures—'Let us have a complete rain.'"

CHAPTER 9

PEACE CENTER

In 1965, a small group of prominent American Jewish businessmen called on Truman in Independence, to obtain his sanction for the building of a monument in his name to commemorate his historic decision to extend American recognition to the State of Israel. Truman was pleased and thanked them for their generous intentions, but he told them that he disapproved of memorials and felt that they belongs to a bygone age.

Before they departed, they visited with me in my office across the hall and told me of their great disappointment at the failure of their mission. They hoped that I could intervene in some way to change HST's mind. I knew that this was impossible, but I was troubled that these men, who came in the spirit of good will, should depart empty-handed. Perhaps something could be salvaged out of it. I knew that the question of peace was always uppermost with the President, and that gave me an idea that might appeal to him. I asked the gentlemen to wait and went to Truman's office to ask him how he would feel about the establishment of an active peace center if this group could underwrite its funding.

The mood of the President suddenly changed; his eyes lighted up and he said, "That's another story. Of course, I would, if you can work it out. But whatever they do about the funding, I don't want it imposed on the public; so be sure not to pass the hat around."

When I rejoined the group, I informed them that President Truman authorized me to propose a plan for the establishment of an international center for the advancement of peace bearing his name, to be situated in an appropriate location in the Holy Land, and that they might return here in two or three weeks with commitments sufficient to underwrite the construction of a facility to house the center. The group accepted the proposal at once with great enthusiasm.

April 14, 1966

Dear Dave:

I am much encouraged by the progress that the Center For
the Advancement of Peace has made in so short a time
toward its important goal.

I hope and expect that the affairs of the Center will be diligently pursued so that it can begin to perform at the earliest
possible moment.

I think it is well understood by all concerned, that the Center,
because of its sensitive nature, will require that its policies
and the range of its operations be carefully coordinated with
this office.

I, therefore, designate you as my personal representative
and, hereby, authorize you to speak and act for me at all
times in all matters relating to the Center that would be of
concern to me. I know that you will, as has been our practice over the years, confer and consult with me on all
important decisions to make sure that my views are fully
considered before they become effective.

You will, of course, represent me on the several boards
that are to guide the affairs of the Center, and the annual
selection of the recipient of the Peace Award.

Sincerely yours,

Honorable David M. Noyes
1052 Tiverton Avenue
Los Angeles, California 90024

They acted swiftly, and in about two weeks, the group informed us that they had twelve pledges of $100,000 each. Three weeks later, this had snowballed to a total of thirty $100,000 pledges. We were told that one industrialist, a prominent Republican, had this to say when he was asked to contribute. "I don't think I would venture ten cents for the possibility of peace in that part of the world, but I will contribute $100,000 in the name of Harry Truman."

Then, there was the case of a prominent merchant and philanthropist who was approached for a contribution with this appeal, "If you like the project, it would cost you $100,000. If you don't, you will have lost only a few minutes of your time."

He replied, "I'll come over and listen to what you have to say, but I can tell you now that it won't cost a cent." When he was informed that it was for a peace project in the name of Harry Truman, he said, "I've heard enough. You've got your $100,000."

The funding campaign was successful beyond all expectations. As the day drew near for the inaugural ceremonies of the Peace Center, everything appeared to augur well for the future of this effort, albeit private, to advance the cause of peace in the name of the man who had done so much to foster it. The date set for the official inauguration of the Truman Center was January 20, 1966. Invitations to participate in the ceremonies were cabled by HST to leaders of other nations. The replies were heartwarming.

President Nassar of Egypt, through his ambassador in Washington, expressed his interest in the purpose of the Center and indicated that he would follow it, its work and policies with care. The response from

President Habib Bourguiba of Tunisia expressed his hopes for an era of peace in that part of the world. The President of Mexico sent his hopeful good wishes. The Philippines designated an ambassador to represent that nation, as did Canada and many others.

The significance of the Truman Center was attested to by the presence of notables from many nations. President Johnson arrived, bringing with him representatives from the Diplomatic Corps, members of Congress, former staff members of the Truman administration, and Chief Justice Warren who, with HST and President Johnson, would be the keynote speakers.

The sanctity of the occasion was evidenced by the participation of representatives from the various religious denominations. All of those who were scheduled to speak on the program had devoted a great deal of thought and effort to articulate their hopes and expectations for the fulfillment of the noble objectives of the Peace Center.

Truman had spent many hours in preparing his statement. Unhappily, he was recovering from a bout of the flu and could not be subjected to the strain of delivering it himself. He called upon me to do it for him, and I read selected portions from his paper.

Statement by Former President of the United States Harry S. Truman at the Inauguration Ceremonies of the Harry S. Truman Center for the Advancement of Peace in the City of Jerusalem, on January 20, 1966, at the Harry S. Truman Library in Independence, Missouri-at 10:00 a.m.

Mr. President,

Mr. Chief Justice,

Distinguished and Honored Guests, and a special greeting to you my very good friends, the Founders of the Center for the Advancement of Peace.

By your acts, and by your presence, you who came here from near and far-have made this day a day of new hope-a day of new promise that the way to peace in our time will yet shine forth from the Promised Land.

You have made this day one of the most important days of my life and I am profoundly grateful to you all.

First, I wish to express our thanks to the President of the United States for his inspiring words of encouragement to our undertaking.

With all of you, I pray that the word will go forth from this Center to all continents—the world of peace and good will to all men.

When I am in the company of the great Chief Justice of the United States, I feel a deep sense of comfort, that the cause of justice, the vigilant protection of our free institutions, is in strong and safe hands. I feel confident that the intent and purpose of the far-seeing founding fathers who drew up the Constitution, are interpreted with firmness and courage. This nation is fortunate to have Chief Justice Earl Warren where he is at this period of our existence as a nation-a period of transition and adjustment to changing new conditions.

We meet in an institution dedicated to the people of all nations. They come here by the tens of thousands-students, teachers, heads of governments, farmers, workers-to learn something of the nature of our free institutions, how we are organized to govern ourselves, and something of the American Presidency-the most powerful, yet the most responsive and self-disciplined office on earth.

We meet at a time in history when the world is best with troubles and hostilities in many places. It is a world in evolution and revolution. An unimaginable catastrophe of a third world war hangs like a dark cloud over all mankind. What so many in places of leadership do not seem to realize is that if petty bickerings and squabbles are not peaceably resolved, the situation could get out of hand-as it has so many times in the past. But the next time, it will not merely [be] a third world conflict-it could well be the last folly of man-likely the last of man on this earth.

There will be no Noah's Ark to save and repopulate the species-the waters will be deadly as well-for any life to survive.

It is, therefore, the first order of responsibility confronting all government leaders under whatever system they choose to live, to determine how to do away with war completely as a way of international life.

No wars can be regarded as inevitable. Wars do not happen by some mystical process emanating from some outer world. Wars are made-man made.

They are made by power hungry adventurers, fanatical zealots, empire builders, false prophets, crusading conquerors or, too often, depraved madmen. They incite, arouse and provoke their subjects to acts of war. In each case there is first an act of war by an aggressor. And, whenever there is an aggressor, inevitably the offended nation must choose its path— surrender or defensive action. Then, the fat is in the fire-and the flames usually spread. The result-death, wounded, disease, hunger, pestilence-and no victory-even to the conquerors. Only misery and retribution await them.

Wars are quick to start-and painfully slow to stop.

In this sense, the United Nations has more than lived up to its reason for existence. It has been effective in putting out or preventing several dangerous brush fires. But there still remains the big question as to whether in this current struggle for power-especially in the area of ideological conflicts-whether the U.N. can be the influence for peace we had hoped that it could be.

I had tried, during my term of office, to place within the U.N. the capability for peace enforcement. To that end, I had offered to place the custody of atomic weapons within the U.N.-in the hope that this action by the United States at a time when we had monopoly of the A-bomb would prevent the proliferation of nuclear weapons-and halt the armaments race. The only condition we attached to this proposal was the right of inspection by the U.N. representatives to prevent cheating.

We have tried in other ways to foster and encourage peace. As the victor we wanted no reparations from the defeated. On the contrary we set out at once to help repair the devastation, to bind the wounds and feed the hungry-friend and foe alike.

There was the Point IV plan, the Marshall Plan and a food program for the hungry: all of these were available to all nations, without distinction. All we expected and all we wanted in return for our efforts and contributions was not territory-no special economic or any other privilege-all we wanted was to help secure the peace-to be done with war-once and for all.

But, it all seems to have been in vain. Memories are short-and appetites for power and glory are insatiable. Old tyrants depart. New ones take their places. Old differences are composed, new differences arise. Old allies become the foe. The recent enemy becomes the friend. It is all very baffling and trying.

For it is all too obvious, that if we do not abolish war <u>on</u> this earth, the surely, one day, war will abolish us <u>from</u> the earth.

But we cannot lose hope, we cannot despair. We must continue our efforts for peace without let-up.

Part of our problem stems from the sudden emergence of many new nations. Part comes from the imposition of new ideologies on vast populations. And still another source of difficulty is attributable to the new means of mass electronic communication in the hands of leaders who are bent on making trouble.

In the meantime, I would venture to suggest a simple solution to all belligerents. Leave your neighbor alone! Do not covet anything that belongs to another people. Let them work out their way and destiny-and do not impose your so-called help unless they ask it and want it.

Perhaps, the ultimate lasting solution to the question of war and peace, will come, when people everywhere begin to realize that the answer is up to them. One day, their voices will be heard especially in nations that now have only one-way communication—from the government to the people.

Let me suggest, however, that it is also important that we prevent internal violence as a means of redressing just grievances in the evolving nations and even here at home.

These we must approach not by acts of suppression but with compassion and understanding. And, I suggest that we attend to these problems with all deliberate speed-to use a celebrated phrase of your Court, Mr. Chief Justice, so that we do not burden succeeding generations with any unfinished and unresolved issues that we, of this generation, are duty-bound to attend to now.

History teaches us many lessons, but too many are in the negative. They only disclose the policies that have been proved wrong and the mistakes that we should not repeat.

Indeed, we should all study our history, but we should not become its prisoners. For history is not always the most dependable guide on how to plan the future. We need to develop our own sense of the future, with new perspectives-new attitudes and open minds.

I hope that the Center for the Advancement of Peace will bring to each and everyone of the Founders the enduring satisfaction of having participate in an undertaking designed to save us from ourselves.

And let me add this personal note. The establishment of the Center for the Advancement of Peace is, to me, a most gratifying experience and I again want to express to you my profound thanks. And, when the day comes-when it is time to close the book of my life-I will be comforted by the hoped that this Center for the Advancement of Peace will become a major source of light and reason toward the achievement of eternal peace.

/s/ Harry Truman

* * * * * * * * *

It is implicit that the President would have a voice in all important decisions regarding the organization of the Center and its operation. Moreover, he wanted it to be an unallied institution, unencumbered in its authority, and in all respects supranational. He further specified that the Board of Trustees be international in scope and made up of five recognized experts in the field of international relations. He suggested Chief Justice Earl Warren for the Chairmanship of the Board of Trustees, and that Trygve Lie, First Secretary General of the United Nations, be included. Both accepted.

Furthermore, the President expected that the Center would not become mired in abstract, academic pursuits of the issues of war and peace, but that it would concentrate on the practical problems in critical areas of housing, agriculture, health, pestilence, and employment.

November 18, 1963

Dear Mr. Chief Justice:

The International Center for the Advancement
of Peace on Mount Scopus which is to bear my
name is nearing completion. An "International
Board of Overseers" composed of distinguished
leaders of many nations will control its policies
and keep it on its designated course.

I would like you to be Chairman of that Board.
I would deeply appreciate it, if you would accept.

With warm regards,

Sincerely yours,

Honorable Earl Warren
The Chief Justice
The Supreme Court of the United States
Washington, D. C.

The site allocated for the Peace Center was situated within the compound of the Hebrew University in Jerusalem. On July 11, 1966, the City of Jerusalem was draped in American flags and banners to welcome Truman for the groundbreaking ceremony. Unfortunately, Truman's doctors declared that it would be too great a risk in his present condition.

Thurgood Marshall, Solicitor General of the United States, (who was soon to become Associate Justice of the Supreme Court), represented president Truman at the ceremony, along with Rose Conway, the President's long time trusted and devoted private secretary. The impressive and solemn formal dedication ceremonies took place in the main auditorium of the University of Jerusalem. I was authorized to present the statement that President Truman had hoped to be able to make in person.

Statement by Former President of the United States Harry S. Truman, to be delivered at the Ground-Breaking Ceremony of the Harry S. Truman Center for the Advancement of Peace, at the Hebrew University in the City of Jerusalem on Monday, July 11, 1966.

I had hoped against hope that I would somehow manage to make the pilgrimage to this ancient city. I have been wanting to come here for a long time-to stand where man's highest aspirations had their earliest beginnings. This part of the world also holds many deep and meaningful associations for me. However, in deference to the wishes of my family, and at the insistence of my physician, it became necessary for me to postpone my visit to Jerusalem until this fall.

In times such as these, I like to think of the enduring relations that have prevailed between Canada and the United States. Our two nations have been living side by side, separated by the longest unfortified common frontier, with no thought of any possible serious trouble developing.

This is not to say that we always see eye to eye on all issues. Differences inevitably arise, even between the friendliest of nations. But we usually have little trouble in resolving our differences as good neighbors respecting each other's sovereign rights ought to do.

There is another noteworthy example of the good neighbor policy to the South of our border. We enjoy a warm and friendly relationship with our esteemed neighbor-the great nation of Mexico. Here too, we get along peacefully and with good feeling, and a healthy mutual respect toward each other.

The distinguished participants who came here from near and far attest to the pressing need of a rallying call to peace. There are growing indications that this Center has an important role and mission to perform as a practical and rational voice of the peacemakers.

I particularly wish to salute the Founders of the Center, who had the vision, the courage, the faith and the humanity to make this institution possible. Their heritage will be the most rewarding satisfaction that can come to any person-the reward of the enduring good deed. They have made this day a high point in my life and I am eternally grateful to each and everyone of them.

We came here to rededicate our means, our skills, our moral and intellectual resources, to a cause that has priority on the minds and hearts of the leaders of all nations.

There are serious trouble spots in the world where tensions are mounting. Unless these are checked and peaceably resolved, they will tend to spread and explode into a war we must not ever let happen.

We cannot dismiss the possibility that the unimaginable catastrophe of a third world war continues to cloud the future of mankind's survival on this earth.

For, if we should be so blind and senseless as to blunder into a third world war the great strides in science and technology and all of man's creative work and progress in culture, the arts, literature, then man and all things living wee be destroyed in a flash and a puff.

It is unthinkable that, with the huge stockpiles of nuclear arsenals, and with missiles with nuclear warheads poised on their pads for instant assault, that there could be any valid reason why any government would refuse to come to terms with its neighbors. To those who would persist in such outdated practices, I would respectfully suggest that they would best serve the interests of their own citizens if they would concern themselves with the problems of world disarmament.

There is no longer any question that disarmament is the one most decisive step we must take to prevent the incident or the miscalculation that could plunge the world to its ultimate death.

Yet, when we talk of disarmament, we are obliged to temper our idealism with practical realism. For there can be no drastic disarmament without the assurance of mutual security, and we must face up to the difficulty that not all nations have so progressed in their development that they stand ready to join the other nations in a program of gradual disarmament.

We can point with some hope and comfort to one important achievement in that direction. I refer, of course, to the organization of the United Nations. It should be our solemn duty to give the United Nations our full, moral and material support to make sure that this peace-fostering organization will have the capability to meet its responsibilities, the most important of which is to discourage those who are quick to resort to armed hostilities.

Indeed, what a crushing burden would be lifted from the backs of men of every nation, if we could at least make a substantial beginning toward disarmament within the framework of the United Nations.

During my term in office as President, I sought to equip the United Nations with the capability for peace enforcement. At the time when our nation was in sole possession of the atomic bomb, we offered to turn over the process and the bomb to the Untied Nations for safekeeping.

It was our thought that by transferring control of the bomb to the United Nations we would help to prevent its eventual proliferation as well as to preclude the possession of the bomb by some latter-day irresponsible adventurer who would use it to threaten other nations into submission.

We know too well of the dangers of a power-crazed fanatic arising seemingly from nowhere to make a new bid for world conquest. History is all too clear on that score.

There was another important consideration behind our offer of the bomb to the United Nations; it was our hope that control of the atomic weapon, by this world peace-keeping organization the United Nations, would act as a brake on the armament race.

The only condition that we attached to our offer was that every nation had to submit to mutual inspection by the United Nations inspectors to prevent cheating.

Our hopes that all nations would respond with an enthusiastic welcome to our move to internationalize the bomb were soon shattered. By invoking its veto, one nation succeeded in nullifying our proposal. And, from that moment on, the nuclear race was on. All that is now history.

As things stand, the "Nuclear Club" has acquired several new members. There are those who insist on acting on their own. In time the number will grown unless the people assert themselves and have their say—and put an end to the production of all atomic weapons and limit the use of nuclear energy to peaceful purposes. This is a decision that cannot be put off much longer. For example, witness the paradox of peace indoctrinated nation, India, having to give serious thought to the production of its own bomb. Although she does not want the bomb, and never did want it, she faces the dilemma of having to meet the threat form those who do have it.

We are at a point in history where it is incumbent upon all governments and their leaders to reflect and ponder carefully before they embark on a road from which there can be no returning. To put it more simply, the best way to prevent a war is not to start one.

And, so we meet here to try to make a fresh start. Here at the Center for the Advancement of Peace we will give serious consideration to any new practical approach that could help to advance the cause of peace. All will be welcome here, who desire to join in our common search for the ways of peace. There are no restrictions as to national origin, ideological commitment or religious differences. Here, hope we will join in the spirit of reason and tolerance to give free and full expression to our hopes and ideals.

At this point I should reaffirm our earlier announcement at the Independence, Missouri inaugural that the annual peace award is now in effect. I prayerfully hope that I shall have the opportunity and satisfaction to greet the person who, in the judgment of the trustees, has been responsible for significantly advancing the cause of peace in this year of war. And please note, that the emphasis is on "significantly advancing."

And, finally, permit me to end on a person note. I have lived a long life and a full life. I have tried to live the good life as best I knew it. When the responsibility was mine, I joined with others to help shape a world that would one day come to enjoy the blessings of peace-with freedom and security and a better life for all.

I continue to have a deep faith in man's nobler side and his rightful destiny; all he needs is to be given a fair chance. This, I believe, to be the essence of the great American dream.

A dream of a world without war, without want, without misery.

The Center for the Advancement of Peace, is now part of that dream.

November 22, 1966

A WISH FOR THE NEW YEAR

By Harry S. Truman

First and foremost, I join with all people of all nations in the wish for an era of peace on this earth.

I wish for an end to acts of violence and belligerence as a way of resolving differences between peoples of opposing ideologies, religions or national origins.

I wish that every leader and spokesman for a government would come to realize that all wars are not only preventable-but that war must be prevented by every available means-lest we one day become involved again in the big war which, in this nuclear age, could well lead to the extinction of all mankind.

I wish that in the coming year, that the United Nations would bestir itself and firm up in a resolute rededication to its high calling and purpose, as the organization charged with the maintenance of world peace.

Then, too, I wish for an end to the tragedy of hunger and starvation which continue to afflict communities in so many places. Progress in agricultural technology and science should now make it possible for us to produce enough food to meet only one the needs of every human being, but a surplus for a continuing stockpile as well.

In recent years we have witnessed remarkable progress in the field of medicine and sanitation, yet disease and pestilence continue to exact a frightful toll in lives. I wish that the benefits of the new discoveries were more available to more people.

And, finally, I wish that the Center for the Advancement of Peace, in the City of Jerusalem, will be erected in the coming year to join with other existing facilities in the solemn engagement of keeping the peace.

* * * * * * * *

Mr. President, Mr. Prime Minister, Members of the Board of Governors, Fellow Founders, Distinguished Guests.

I wish that it had been possible for me to join with you in the dedication and commitment of the Center we will build here on Mount Scopus to the fulfillment of man's anguishing hope for a world at peace.

I wanted to be here with you on this historic site to raise my voice in an urgent plea for a restoration of peace on this earth, while there is yet time. But I am at a time of life when it is no longer advisable for me to venture on extensive travel and it is, for that reason, that I am addressing myself to you in this manner.

We have all come to realize that time is running out and that events are moving swiftly in a direction which, if not arrested, could lead us into the catastrophe of a Third World War.

I am sure that it is no secret to any of you that President Truman since leaving the White House, has had a continuing and consuming interest in the cause of peace, as he has been deeply troubled whenever there occurred an outbreak of hostilities in any part of the world. It is understandable why he has not been happy with the trend of world affairs and the seeming inability by the United Nations organization to function effectively in its peace keeping role.

"...And finally, I wish to make it clear that I did not consent to associate myself with this Center without giving the proposal deep thought and careful consideration. I have always had a particular interest in this part of the world, where so much of civilization and spiritual development originated, where invading conquerors have caused so much bloodshed and destruction and where religious crusades have left their deep scars. Yet, I believe that at the Center we can make a modest, practical, approach to help allay the threats, the tensions and fears that persist in this ancient land. Here, as in other explosive areas, peace is desperately needed lest the situation get out of hand. And if it should get out of control we know what the consequences would be if that should come to pass. In the name of all that is sacred to a common humanity, let us end the folly and cruelty of war.

I think it is necessary that I make it clear that in this Center we shall not be primarily concerned with the academic aspects of the issues of war and peace. Rather we expect to direct our efforts toward the practical issues of the problems of peace and the many opportunities that we shall develop to serve in helping to lift some of the burdens and miseries that now afflict so many human beings in so many parts of the world.

* * * * * * * * * * * * *

While I was in Jerusalem, I received word that Prime Minister Levi Eshkol was so pleased with the prospects for the Truman Center that he had requested his foreign office to prepare a suitable statement on the subject which he would make in his forthcoming travels of the African nations. The inherent dangers in such an approach, I knew, would imperil the future of the project. It would look as though it were an Israeli facility being projected by its Prime Minister, thus subverting Truman's plan for an unallied institution. I arranged an immediate appointment with the Prime Minister and sat down with him for a few hours. I urged him to take a broader view of the program for the Center and reminded him of President Truman's hopes that we would create here a citadel beholden to no one nation, and to which antagonists and protagonists alike would feel free to come, to discuss, to reason, and to resolve.

At first, Prime Minister Eshkol held fast to his plan. But, when he finally realized that we had to keep our sights on the "big door" to peace, so that Israel, too, could make use of it, he picked up the phone to his foreign office and ordered that his intended statements on the Peace Center be cancelled. I came away much relieved, for if the Prime Minister had insisted on going through with his plan, the Center would have been doomed even before it had started.

On June 5, 1967, the "Six-Day War" erupted. In its wake, "The Center" found a new home atop the historic Mt. Scopus. President Truman had always talked of this as the ideal site for a center for peace. On March 24, 1968, it was dedicated with a statement which I read for President Truman. Work was begun to erect a suitable home for the "Center."

The exterior was covered with a pink marble indigenous to that area, (a sample of which I carried back to President Truman), and the interior was equipped with all of the necessary facilities to accommodate its staff and visiting dignitaries.

As the building was reaching completion, there were disturbing rumors that the original purpose of the Center was being subverted and redirected from its intended function. Then one day, we received at Independence, a communication informing President Truman that a new board of directors had just been elected, consisting of faculty members of the University of Jerusalem and representatives of the founding members. The fundraisers had staged a coup. The university had appropriated the Peace Center, and it looked as though the danger that I had managed to avert in 1966 with Prime Minister Eshkol had come full circle. In that connection, President Truman asked me to write to Dr. Herzog and to explain to him why had had been experiencing disillusionment and disappointment at the misdirection of the Center.

August 27, 1969

Dear Dr. Herzog:

I have been pretty much on the move since my return, in relation to the matters I touched on with you as they concerned the Truman Center.

It might be in order briefly to review the original concept of the Center and the preconditions that decided Mr. Truman to become actively associated with it.

The first of these was that the Center assume an activist's role in the human environmental aspects of peace, such as contemplated in his Point IV program, but, of course, on a lesser scale. That we were to concern ourselves with the plight of all who are reduced to subhuman conditions of existence.

The second stipulation had to do with the areas of research and special group discussion dealing with the ways and means of making the Center an effective voice for peace, as well as an instrument in ways practical. But it was clearly stated that the Center would resist being overcommitted to academic disciplines.

Since its founding in January 1966, the Center became mired in trivia, irrelevant activities and adrift of its intended course.

Mr. Truman decided thereupon that he could not allow this state of affairs to continue, and he acted. He addressed a message to Mr. Harman and copies to each of the Founders, expressing his disappointment and requesting a prompt correction. This action appears to have brought everyone concerned up sharply and we are now working our way back to the original purpose.

President Harman has been a tower of strength throughout and has provided a steady hand to the reaffirmation of Mr. Truman's concept of the Center's role.

It has been our good fortune to engage the interest and participation of Chief Justice Earl Warren when he accepted Mr. Truman's invitation to assume the Chairmanship of the International Board of Overseers of the Center. Serving with him as board members are Mr. Hubert H. Humphrey, Mr. Lester Pearson and Dr. James Bryant Conant. Others will be added from time to time.

These two activities will engage the International Board's concern as soon as the required documents are produced.

The first will deal with a certain new concept of good and economical housing to which we will have the rights for the Middle-East as a start. This activity will be activated under the direct sponsorship of Chief Justice Warren and the International Board.

The second involves a sensitive and delicate mission, informally arranged, to the heads of certain states to establish for the Center a hoped for receptivity as a supranational unbiased and politically unincumbered facility devoted to the advancement of peace as a universal forum, where reason and man's nobler instincts will have a calming voice upon those who incite to violence.

I was deeply stirred in my meetings with you, and am looking forward to an early revisit.

With all best,

Sincerely,

David M. Noyes

Dr. Yaacov Herzog
Director
General Office of the Prime Minister
Jerusalem, Israel

135

The President was so shocked and offended at this usurpation of the Center, that he at once disassociated himself from it. He requested that a new facility be established in the United States where it could function in an atmosphere of total neutrality and, to that end, the fund that had been raised for the Center be reassigned. But it was all for naught. The fundraisers insisted on having a majority representation on the American board. The original intent of a new approach to peace in the name of Harry Truman had been reduced to an exercise in fundraising and petty chauvinism.

Supreme Court of the United States
Washington D. C. 20543

November 2, 1970

CHAMBERS OF
HEF JUSTICE WARREN
RETIRED

Mr. David M. Noyes,
Harry S. Truman Library,
Independence, Missouri 64050.

Dear Mr. Noyes:

I trust you will not feel that I have been treating lightly your
letter of August 10, 1970, concerning the proposed Truman International
Center for Peace.

I dictated an answer to your letter on September 29th. However,
in order to test the reasonableness of the statements I made in it, I
sent a copy to Mr. Benjamin H. Swig of San Francisco for his comment.
He was the only one of the contributors whom I knew sufficiently well to
solicit his confidential opinion in the matter.

Time has passed, but he now advises me that he agrees completely
with my letter, and that he has talked to you concerning it. I, too, have
thought about it in the interim, and am more convinced than ever that if
President Truman's Peace Center is to be the success you and I hope it
will be there must be a complete separation of it from the University and
from Israeli investments.

I would appreciate it if you would tell the President that my sole
concern is the reaction to a continued subordination or even relationship
with any nation in this troubled part of the world.

With best wishes, I am

Sincerely,

CHAMBERS OF
CHIEF JUSTICE WARREN
RETIRED

Mr. David M. Noyes,
Harry S. Truman Library,
Independence, Missouri 64050.

Dear Mr. Noyes:

Excessive travel has prevented me from responding to your letter of a few weeks ago. Its importance called for a more prompt answer.

I do want you to know that I agree with it thoroughly. There is no other basis than that outlined by you through which we could possibly do justice to the desires of President Truman and worthy of his aspirations for a just peace in a troubled world. Nothing but a complete separation from outside interests and a fresh, independent start would give the project that degree of objectivity which would convince people in all parts of the world of the sincerity of our endeavors.

Please convey my fervent best wishes to President and Mrs. Truman for a very happy holiday season, and with like sentiments to you, I am

Sincerely,

[signature]

Dear Mr. Chief Justice:

I am most grateful to you for taking the time and trouble to assess the posture of the Truman Peace Center in light of its prior involvement with the Hebrew University complex.

Your letter arrived at a propitious moment as I was meeting with a group representing the Founders for the purpose of finalizing legally and morally our total severance.

The meeting was a disappointment as is revealed in the enclosed copy of the letter I wrote to General Goldstein, who presided and was equally unhappy at the direction the meeting took.

It would appear that unless these people let us completely alone, we shall have to make a fresh start and go it alone.

With all best,

Sincerely,

David M. Noyes

Honorable Earl Warren
Supreme Court of the United States
Washington, D. C. 20343

CC X - Chief Justice Warren

With that development, Chief Justice Warren resigned from the Center. The President's patience was exhausted. It was a distasteful experience to him and to his family, and was hardly a beneficial prescription for his failing health.

A call was put through from the Truman House to Charles Murphy, former Truman White House counsel, requesting that he notify the Internal Revenue Agency to cancel the application pending there for the establishment of a non-profit, tax exempt foundation, "The Harry S. Truman Center for the Advancement of Peace."

Ronald Appel, Esq.
Appel and Goldman
21 East 40th Street
New York, New York

Dear Mr. Appel:

It is my painful duty to inform you that the compromise
resolution concerning the restructuring of the Truman
International Center for the Advancement of Peace to its
original intent and purpose, came too late.

Repeated warnings had been issued over a period of more
than four years to those in charge as well as the Founders
that the delays and bargaining tactics being employed would
inevitably place the Center in grave jeopardy, but to no
avail. Finally, in a last desperate appeal for a compromise
settlement, we came to an agreement which we regarded as
the best of a bad bargain.

On March 27th there was a meeting in Independence at which
the future of the Center was reviewed. As a consequence of
the position taken by Justice Earl Warren, Chairman designate of the International Board, and others, among them
members of the family, the decision was made to terminate
all activities and plans relating to the Center.

Please, therefore, take all the necessary steps to effectuate
the aforesaid decision.

On the personal side, I wish to express my appreciation for
your help and good efforts.

                                        Sincerely,

                                        David M. Noyes

The memorial that President Truman had rejected so vigorously in the first place, stands today on Mt. Scopus—Truman's name on the outside, but not on the inside.

CHAPTER 10

TRUMAN AND EISENHOWER

When General Dwight David Eisenhower became the Republican candidate for the Presidency, a marked change came over him. He became a hard core partisan and campaigned as one, even though he had never worked at party politics. But, despite it all, to a great many people, he could do no wrong or say no wrong. Such was his popularity that no matter how stumbling and ineffectual his campaigning, he was riding a winning trend.

President Truman was, of course, totally committed to Adlai Stevenson as nominee of his party; he regarded him as superior to Eisenhower by intellect and experience. Stevenson's distinguished performance as Governor of Illinois together with his services in the State Department were the essential qualifications as stepping stone to the Presidency.

Despite Eisenhower's political conversion, Truman's personal liking for him remained unimpaired. Then something happened in the political arena to jolt HST into a violent resentment to the General. It happened in Milwaukee where Eisenhower was making a political appearance. Joining him on the platform was, of all people, the notorious character assassin, Senator Joe McCarthy. Curiously, the presence of McCarthy posed no embarrassment to Ike.

McCarthy used the occasion to level a vicious attack on the character and patriotism of General George C. Marshall. He not only impugned his patriotism, but dared to go so far as to accuse him of being a Communist sympathizer. Yet, inexplicably, Eisenhower just stood there lifting nary a finger against this diatribe and, by his mute presence, gave credibility to these outrageous pronouncements against his one time benefactor. The old cliche that politics makes strange bedfellows was well illustrated on this black day in Milwaukee.

When President Truman first got word of it, he was incredulous. But, when it was confirmed on the newsticker, HST was angered and offended, and from that moment on, he was determined to go on the attack. He made use of every opportunity to level sharp critical barbs at Eisenhower.

Dear Bete :— I enjoyed the plane
ride with you for two reasons.
One was the ride and the instruction and the other was to learn
your viewpoint on McCarthy.

When he was in the navy I'm
told by a man on the same ship
with him that he stumbled over
a station and hurt his leg. After
he became a Senator he forced
a navy Admiral to give him a
medal for it.

In his speech at Wheeling
West Virginia he charged that
there were 105 Communists
in the State Department and

not one was found. You'll
say that Alger Hiss was one.
He was not convicted as a
Communist. His book I think
proves that hysteria cause his
conviction just as it did the
witches in New England with
Cotton Mather.

He stood on the platform
in Milwaukee with Jenner and
Eisenhower and called General
Marshall a traitor. If the General
is a traitor so am I and the
country's in a hell of a fix.
I gave Ike a good lecturing one
that at Colorado Springs the

146

day after it was done and
Ike's been frustrated about
it ever since. Now Bake you
friend McCarthy is one of the
biggest lying demogogues this
country ever produced. He is
in a class by himself because
he's the only Senator in history
who was given a vote of elation.

I was somewhat surprised
when you said the working
press were half commy be-
cause they believe in the rights
of the every day man. Hearst is a
man in class by himself and it

is in my class. If he'd had
his May 1793 in Paris would
have been a picnic to what
we'd have had in 1930..

Eisenhower's campaign was a sorry performance. He did not present the issues with clarity nor his position with comprehension. But, to his audiences, it made no difference; he could do no wrong. The combination of the "father image," the victorious, glamorous general, and the public's "I Like Ike" predisposition made him indeed a formidable opponent for Stevenson to overcome.

However, Stevenson had much going for him, too. His urbanity, gentle humor, polished literary style, and credibility began to take hold, and halfway through the campaign, there appeared to be developing a reversal in the trend of the election. This development was completely unforeseen in the Eisenhower camp, and a measure of panic set in. An expert journalist was brought in to help, and he came up with a timely and effective prescription. He focused in on Korea as a major issue, and Eisenhower made quick use of it at the first opportunity. In an appearance in Detroit, he said, "If elected, I will go to Korea."

The Korean War was on the public's mind. It was a troublesome, nagging engagement, waged under the auspices of the United Nations, and Ike's declaration caught the public's attention. That device was not new. Churchill used it in a similar way in a hard fought bid for re-election when, in the closing days of the contest, he announced. "If elected, I will go to Moscow." It worked.

Soon after that turn in the fortunes of the campaign, Stevenson's spirit began to falter. He wound up his campaign on a shakey, irresolute, and dispirited mood.

One would have expected that on Inaugural Day, Eisenhower would have worn his broadest smile on this, the nadir of his distinguished career.

But, he did not rise to it. He was still smoldering from the tongue lashing administered to him by Truman during the course of the campaign. For one thing, he defied tradition by wearing a Homberg instead of the customary top hat. For another, he refused to join the outgoing President in a brief repast which was another established custom, and sat in the open car, rejecting Truman's invitation to come inside. He sat there waiting for Truman to come out. Truman accommodated and sat down beside him in the car. As they drove to the Capitol, Eisenhower made it clear that he was still not on speaking terms with Truman. Along the way, looking glaringly at Truman, he managed to blurt out, "Who is responsible for ordering my son to the Inaugural?"

The President replied, "By order of the President of the United States."

Stony silence followed. From that day on, the relationship between these two men appeared to be permanently breached.

What happens to
a President when
he goes back to his
native community.
On January 20th 1953,
the newly elected President
was sworn in at 12:05 P.M.

When that was done I moved
off the platform, as I should
have done, as my successor
was now President of the
United States.

When it came time to leave
the White House, Mrs. Truman
and I waited for the New President
to come to 1600 Pennsylvania for
a formal luncheon. Well he did
not come. After waiting for
some time I went out on the

151

front porch of the White House
and found a sleek passenger car – with
Ike in it. I waited on the front
porch and finally he came up the
steps and I moved into the car –
on the right side now which he tried
to move me. Why, as the man, who
thought he saw the Archbishop of Canterbury on the platform of the sub-
way (the tube as the Britishers
call it), did he think that.

Well the object of his vision
had a long tailed coat of the time,
gaiters and a flat top hat.
His partner told him to go
and ask if he was looking
at the Archbishop of Canterbury.
He was a little timid but

152

he went over to the gentle-
man and asked his question-
The purported Archbishop
looked at him and made
this remark - so I'm told -
"Why you lousy commy-
mon son of the lower class,
it's none of your bloody
business"
My friend returned to
his companion and said -
"Now we'll never know"
So I'll never know what
caused Ike to act as he did.
Probably a long

Truman continued to be much concerned about the continuity of our foreign policy. He undertook to write a series of commentaries on the conduct of our foreign policy under President Eisenhower, sometimes critical but ofttimes in support.

One day a call came through from Allen Dulles (then head of the CIA) to Truman in Kansas City. He wanted an appointment to discuss an urgent matter on behalf of President Eisenhower. When Dulles arrived by special plane in great secrecy, he brought with him the text of a speech that Eisenhower planned to make to the United Nations Assembly the following day. Dulles explained that President Eisenhower was anxious for any comments and suggestions Truman might offer. Handing the manuscript to Truman, he said, "By the way, even my brother (John Foster Dulles, Secretary of State) has not seen it."

Truman immediately returned the manuscript to Dulles, saying, "I will be among those who will be eagerly listening to the President's statement, but I don't want to prejudge it. If I did, I would be precommitted. After I hear the speech with everybody else, and if I approve of it, I will be only pleased to say so. In the event that I don't, then I shall feel free to speak my mind."

In later years, after he was out of office, Eisenhower took special pains to show that he held President Truman in the highest respect. The old friendship between them was rekindled. This restoration of the good feeling between them pleased Truman greatly.

At the time of the Kennedy funeral, Ike called on Truman at the Blair House to ask if they might ride together to the Kennedy services. In spite of the tragic circumstances, this meeting radiated the warm relationship as of yore.

Eisenhower was in the mood for reminiscing. He recalled the many missions that he fulfilled under President Truman, their many meetings when he was Army Chief of Staff, and their close personal and official relationship when he was placed in charge of NATO. At no time did he refer to his own Presidency, as if for the moment, he had forgotten that he, too, had held that office.

In another incident, the two former Presidents were scheduled to meet in New York for a United Nations award in their honor. President Truman was ailing and at that time, traveling for him would have been a hardship. Eisenhower accommodated President Truman by coming to Kansas City for the affair. I accompanied HST to the affair at the Muehlbach Hotel where the two former presidents had another pleasant reunion.

At the awards ceremony, Eisenhower who spoke first took a considerable time for his address, but he used the occasion to include some kind comments about Truman. When Truman rose to speak, he practiced his usual brevity. Looking straight at Ike, he said, "When the peace project in which I am so interested, is completed and functioning, you and I can both retire." (The Peace Center to which President Truman referred was The Harry S. Truman International Center for the Advancement of Peace on Mt. Scopus in Jerusalem.)

January 23, 1957

Dear Dave:

I appreciated your note of the 21st, and I am
enclosing a copy of the statement I issued on Ike's
message of the 21st.

I am told it went into all the newspapers. The
Kansas City Star published it on the front page, believe
it or not.

Sincerely yours,

Harry Truman

Hon. David M. Noyes
9489 Dayton Way
Beverly Hills, California

Statement by former President of the United States
Harry S. Truman on President Eisenhower's Message of January 21
1957.

I have carefully read the President's Message. It is a nice collection of beautiful words. It is very strong for home and mother and for world peace, just as we all are, but I see no plan of action outlined in the Message.

Peace in this present troubled world can be obtained only by action on the part of the free world, and it will require the leadership of the United States to accomplish that action. I see no reference to action in the Message. Neither do I see any idea for relief for the farm population; nor do I see any effort to straighten out the finances of the Government and restore building opportunities for returned soldiers and sailors and the other people who want to build modest homes. No effort is being made to stop the gouging of people who are anxious to obtain loans for small business and for building purposes. The money lenders are at their old tricks of gouging the applicants for loans by commissions.

I am sorry about this, because I was hopeful that an active and militant approach to these matters would be made by the President. He is the only source from which leadership in these matters can come.

HARRY S. TRUMAN
FEDERAL RESERVE BANK BUILDING
KANSAS CITY 6, MISSOURI

Sept 10 '55

Dear Dave:—

Here's the Chicago speech. I had the coldest audience this side of the penguins in the Ross Sea — but they came across with an ovation at the end that the penguins would n't have done but Democrats, Jews, Negroes and poor people always do.

Evidently sold 'em a bill of goods. Wish you'd been there to keep me from swelling up too big.

Hope all's well with you

Sincerely,

H.S.T.

158

The following address was made by former President of the United States Harry S. Truman at noon on Friday, September 9, 1955, in the Grand Ballroom of the Conrad Hilton Hotel, Chicago, Illinois, at a luncheon meeting of the Executives' Club of Chicago.

I want to talk to you today about the foreign policy and national defense of the United States.

I am not going to talk primarily as a Democrat, although all of you know that I am a Democrat-and proud of it. I am going to talk as a former President of the United States who learned some important lessons from hard experience.

At the end of World War II, this country took the great step of joining a world organization of nations to keep the peace. Russia joined this organization, too, and assumed the solemn obligation to live in peace with other countries and not to use force in settling disputes. At Yalta and at Potsdam, Russia made promises to join in restoring peace and freedom to the world, and to help bind up the wounds of the war. In spite of all our difficulties with Russia, before and during the war-in spite of all her past crimes and outrages-we hoped that the Soviet leaders would keep these solemn promises which they had made openly and before the whole world. If they had kept those promises and had lived up to their signed agreements, the foundations of peace would have been permanently laid. Things would have worked out for the peace of the world-peace of the world for which we have honestly worked-peace of the world about which the Soviets have talked sweetly, and then sabotaged.

As time went on, we found that the Soviet leaders had no intention of living up to their commitments. To them, promises were merely propaganda for window dressing. The real Russian policy was to extend communist imperialism to the whole world, country by country. And the Russian leaders saw their great chance in the postwar world, because of the economic weakness, the devastation, the disease, poverty and war weariness that afflicted nearly all the countries in the world except our own. So Stalin and his totalitarian machine set to work to divide, subvert, overthrow and engulf the nations that had so recently helped to save the Russians from Hitler.

As it became clear that this communist conspiracy was a grave and increasing threat to free men everywhere, we realized we had to build up the strength of the free world to check this threat and turn it back. This was a hard and costly decision to take so soon after an exhausting world war. But it was a right decision. Freedom is worth preserving whatever the cost. It is always worth preserving. This great nation of ours has fought, bled, and its young men have died for freedom in times past, and I believe we always will stand up and fight for freedom, no matter what the cost.

We increased the size and strength of our Army, Navy, Air Force and Marine Corps. We entered into regional pacts and defense agreements with other free nations to strengthen our mutual defense. We greatly increased our appropriations for defense and expanded our facilities for producing defense needs. To meet outright aggression in Korea, we joined with other free countries under the banner of the United Nations to uphold the Charter of the United Nations.

Our aim in this great national effort was to defend ourselves and the other free nations against the threat of communist conquest-and to do it without bringing on the terrible catastrophe of another world war. It was not easy to pursue this course. We had the isolationists and the appeasers who were saying that what goes on in the rest of the world is no business of ours, and that we should stand still and let the communist tide roll forward. We had the jingoists who were calling for a preventive war and saying, "Strike now-drop the atomic bomb, and smash the enemy at the core." They had no idea what they were asking for.

But we did not follow the advice of either of these radical blocs. We continued on the course we believed to be right. We built up our strength-and that of our friends and we built it up in every way possible, militarily, diplomatically and economically. We did not take up arms until we were attacked-and even then we managed to limit the fighting to one place. We did not become involved in World War III. We stayed with the right way, even if it was the hard way.

I take great pride in what we did-for the pressures were great, and partisan politics was rife. A lot of people who knew better played on misunderstandings and fears and got themselves elected to high office. But we stood firm against involvement in World War III-always hoping for world peace.

We stood firm because we believed that if we continued our efforts to build up our strength and keep the leadership of a united free world, the totalitarians would ultimately have to back down. We believed that when the free world became strong enough, the leaders of communism would recognize the futility of continued attacks, and the dangers of their policy to themselves. And then, we thought, there would be a change in their policies, and they might abandon their strategy of conquest. This was the objective, the hope, that guided our efforts in the years between 1947 and 1952.

It may be that this time of change has now arrived. Perhaps the objective we have been pursuing during these anxious years is at hand-our policy of achieving peace through strength may be beginning to yield concrete results. I certainly hope that is the case. However, it is not now possible to tell with certainty, and it probably will not be possible for a long time to come.

At any rate, the communists have in recent months seemed, on the surface at least, to desire a lessening of world tensions. Undoubtedly, Stalin's death has upset many Russian plans. But what its ultimate significance may be-its ultimate effect on Soviet policy-none of us is wise enough to know. We cannot tell what the real intentions of the new Soviet leaders are. We should not only listen attentively to what they say, but observe most carefully what they actually do.

At present, conferences are being held between the East and the West. These conferences are extremely important. They are an essential part of the process of testing out the true intentions of the communists. The men who represent us in these conferences have a very difficult task-a task which requires wisdom and courage and a very discriminating judgment. They must be ready to take advantage of every genuine opportunity to advance the cause of peace with justice and freedom, but at the same time they must avoid the fatal pitfalls of appeasement. To seize upon the one and avoid the other is not easy. To avoid appeasement has been the effort of eminent statesmen in our time. Their failures in the last generation brought upon us the horrors of a Second World War. God forbid that we should ever have another world war in this nuclear age.

This, then, is our situation:

We must and should confer with the Russians.

We must and should look for peaceful solutions-but never at the price of justice and freedom.

And, above all, we must keep up our guard. It is very easy, when the air is filled with sweet reasonableness, to begin to relax a little. It is exceedingly easy, but it can also be awfully fatal. We must be sure that while we talk peace, the balance of power does not shift against the free world. We must be sure that while we talk of peace, the peoples of the free world do not lose their faith in freedom and fall prey to subversion and tyranny.

Now I want to talk to you about keeping up your guard. This is a big job and a hard and expensive one.

In the first place, we should maintain an attitude of considerable skepticism as to communist promises. Experience teaches us that we should never do anything to weaken our own position solely in reliance upon a communist promise. To justify action on our part, their deeds must match their promises.

Secondly, we should keep up the strength and readiness of our defense forces-and should increase that strength and readiness in those areas where we have not yet achieved the levels which the maintenance of world peace requires. The build-up of our armed forces which was begun during my administration has given us a very powerful military establishment. The present administration has seen fit to cut it down below the goals which we had established, but it still represents very great military strength. I think that strength has had much to do with brining about the attitude of apparent reasonableness on the part of the communists, and thus is achieving a result we had hoped it would. This is further proof of a fact that has been demonstrated many times-the communists do respect strength. If we value peace and freedom, we must be strong.

We cannot be complacent about the military forces we now have-far from it. In fact, the recent disclosures concerning Soviet aircraft development and production raise very serious questions concerning the adequacy of our own forces. Responsible authorities tell us that we are losing ground to the Soviet Union in air power. Both in terms of their power to defend themselves against attack and their power to strike blows of annihilation against our cities, they are making enormous gains. We are losing the margin of leadership we had built up a few years ago. The implications of these facts are enormous and dreadful.

There is nothing in the world today, so far as I know, which will justify permitting this situation to continue.

Peaceful words from behind the iron curtain do not justify it. And certainly it cannot be justified on the ground that we are not able to do more than we are doing. That is too obvious for argument.

The condition of our strength in the air is not the only cause for alarm. The Congress recently showed its concern when it voted-over administration opposition-to appropriate funds needed to avoid cuts in the Marine Corps. I hope very much that this money will be used for the purpose for which it was appropriated.

And if somebody wants to bring up the time I impounded some funds under somewhat similar circumstances, just remember what I told you in the beginning about learning some lessons the hard way.

General Matthew Ridgway, who recently retired as Army Chief of Staff, has expressed grave and well-considered concern over cuts in our ground forces. This was brushed aside as parochialism. If that's what it is, I want to say here and now that I'm from the same parish as General Ridgway.

I think the cuts in our ground forces are unjustified and most dangerous at the present time. These cuts stem back to the basic fallacy of the doctrine of so-called "massive retaliation." The last thing in the world we want to see is massive retaliation by us or against us-in fact, if it ever comes to pass, it will probably be the last thing in the world we ever do see. We want to avoid limited war as well as unlimited war. But we must not get into a position where we shall be obliged to fight an unlimited war or surrender because we have denied ourselves the means of fighting a limited war.

The power of massive retaliation is important-indeed, it is essential as a deterrent to outright international aggression. It is a vital part of the shield we must have to help defend ourselves and our friends while we establish conditions for a just and enduring peace in the world.

But the power of massive retaliation alone is far from enough. Our principal reliance for actively advancing our cause should be on non-military means-on strengthening our economic and cultural ties with other free nations-or working with them to improve the living conditions of mankind. But military strength is vitally important, too, and the kind of military strength that will do the most to help establish a just and enduring peace without the world destruction of a nuclear war is represented by ground forces on the spot.

You have a policeman on the beat to prevent trouble from starting.

You don't send the riot squad out until things have gotten pretty bad.

In the age of nuclear weapons, if you reach the stage where you have to call out the riot squad, then it may be too late to save much from the ruins. *(*Insert): I have been very much disturbed for some time by the administration's policy of crippling the national defense program to hold expenditures down. We have reports of even further cuts in the national defense of the country and the free world, for a politically inspired plan.*

I hope these reports are not true. Cut in the national defense program to save the free world would cause great danger to our safety here at home and would [be] disasterous to our friends and former allies. The safety of ourselves and our allies is too great a sacrifice to make on the alter of that great political "balanced budget."

The budget can be balanced, our safety secured and the free world saved if you are willing to make the dollar sacrifice and pay for it.

In short, I think it is a cardinal principle that in the negotiations with the communists in which we are now engaged, armed strength and not armed weakness will command their respect. Our armed forces are the backbone of that strength, and these forces are certainly no stronger than they need to be in the rugged world of today-indeed, in some respects they are not yet strong enough.

Of course, we would all like to see a different world-a peaceful and disarmed world. I have always worked for disarmament-for the reduction and control of arms. My administration placed practical proposals for disarmament before the United Nations and worked diligently for their adoption. But we always insisted-and I still insist-that we must have effective, enforceable, and balanced disarmament that rests on more than paper promises.

I want to see the world disarmed under United Nations control and inspection which cannot be circumvented or evaded.

To achieve that kind of world-or even to make progress toward it-we must not unilaterally scrap or weaken the present balance of armed strength we have worked so hard to build up.

The current negotiations may go on for a long time. If they are to yield constructive results, I think they <u>must</u> go on for a long time. During all this time, we must be vigilant to keep the free world strong and able to defend itself. Otherwise, the communist leaders may never give up their aggressive designs against the free nations-or they may welch on their promises as they have done before.

Moreover, the balance of power in this troubled world rests not on arms alone, but on people as well. That brings me to the third point which we must bear in mind during what may be a protracted period of negotiations with the communists. That is that we must not relax but must continue and increase our efforts to remove the blights of poverty, disease and ignorance which cause people yearning for a free and better life to yield to the blandishments of totalitarian ideas.

Let us not forget that communism got its start and its hold in Russia and China because those countries were cut off from the main streams of political and economic progress in the last century. It is our responsibility and our interest to see that neglected people in underdeveloped areas do not lose their faith in freedom and fall prey to subversion and tyranny. Point Four and related programs must go forward while there is yet time.

My friends, I do not want to throw a damper on the hopes that have been raised for progress toward peace.

On the other hand, I would not have us forget the lessons of the past. I would not have us take an easy road that leads to disaster. This is why I have raised this note of caution here today.

Do not expect too much too fast. Do not be impatient. Do not clamor for the dismantling of our armed forces. Don't let the budget cutters dismantle them either. Remember, our armed forces are still our shield against disaster. [Remember, too, that any nation which values its freedom in this interdependent world must be concerned with the needs and well-being of other nations. And remember this, we are talking about something very much more important than your income tax rate.

It will cost money to keep America free-much money. And it will take sacrifices that money cannot buy. But it is worth every bit of the cost.

The international picture is not going to change from black to white over night. Anyone who tries to tell you that it can or will is either badly misinformed or guilty of a fraud.

Let us all resolve now that we will do our part to see this thing through to the end-that we will do it the right way even if that is a long and hard way. In the end, that is the best way-in fact, it is the only way-to peace with freedom and justice-and that, my friends, is the only kind of peace worth having.

CHAPTER 11

ADLAI STEVENSON AND MR. TRUMAN

In the summer of 1952, Bill Hillman and I were asked by the President to join him at his vacation hideaway at the submarine base in Key West, Florida. Bill, at that time, was working on a volume authorized by HST, entitled, <u>Mr. President</u>. The reason for wanting the volume published at that particular time, (on the eve of his completion of his term of office), was described in his own words, "I want the people to know the Presidency as I have experienced it, and I want them to know me as I am."

Bill regarded this assignment as a highly privileged trust, and he felt duty bound to make the best of it. Knowing of my personal commitment to the President, he enlisted my help. I knew the importance the President ascribed to it, and I accepted.

The first day of our visit with the President was given over mostly to pleasantries, dining and chatting with his staff. The next day, as we were getting ready to work on the book, the President sent word that he wanted to have a private meeting with us in his living quarters. When we joined him, he said that he wanted to make sure that we were not within the hearing of anyone.

He opened up on the subject that had been on his mind for quite some time. "Now that I am nearing the end of my term, who is there who would be the best qualified to continue with the policies and programs we have inaugurated?"

He regarded Chief Justice Vinson as that person endowed with all the basic qualifications for that office. Vinson had served in all three branches of the government with distinction; he had a strong will and a good mind to make the right decisions; he was always in balance; his integrity was beyond question, and he would not stoop to political expediency; and his broad knowledge of history would serve him well. After he had made that assessment, President Truman revealed to us that he recently had sounded out Vinson on the prospects of making himself available for the nomination, but to Truman's great disappointment, Vinson was determined to remain on the Court.

With his first choice unavailable, HST disclosed that he had surveyed the field for an acceptable and electable candidate, and the only one who came close to measuring up was Adlai Stevenson, Governor of Illinois. He said that he had followed Stevenson's performance as Governor, and he thought he had done an excellent job. He also took note of the fact that one of Stevenson's forebearers had been a Vice President of the United States.

In the meantime, Senator Estes Kefauver's appetite for the office and his energetic moves in that direction caused Truman much concern. He felt that Kefauver lacked the essential stature and requirements for that office.

By nature and commitment, Truman was deeply steeped in the flow of history. It would be completely out of character for him to close the doors on his administration and walk off in carefree detachment. There was much yet to be accomplished in bringing world peace to fruition; there was much yet to be done on the homefront in the areas of employment, public health, civil rights and education. The next occupant of the White

House had to be a person equal to the task. That is why Truman was so preoccupied with the question of succession to the office of the Presidency.

As we were about to leave, Truman surveyed both of us with a question, "Have I overlooked anyone?"

We said in unison, "Yes, you, Mr. President."

"I think the people are in a mood for a change," was his reply.

The more he thought of it, the more Truman became convinced that Stevenson was the best visible candidate. He met with Stevenson at the Blair House and again urged him to declare his candidacy. Stevenson would not be persuaded; he was non-committal as he left, and this remained his attitude right up to the night of the convention.

I came to the convention to keep an eye on developments for the President who was having his annual check-up at Walter Reed Hospital in Washington. As things were shaping up, it was obvious that the convention was in a state of disorganization. With Barkley in the running, and Stevenson persisting as the reluctant candidate, Kefauver could come off the winner. In light of these developments, I telephoned a message to the White House to be delivered by hand to the President's bedside at Walter Reed. The text of the message is enclosed.

July 19, 1952

MEMORANDUM TO THE PRESIDENT

I have carefully checked trends and undercurrents at Chicago.

Find no significant change in basic preferences. You are still predominantly first — with Governor Stevenson the only solid alternate.

Barkley has tradition and sentiment with him. But even with McKinney's and Biffel's efforts and the word that he is your personal choice, there is still a feeling that he won't stand up. I see all sorts of indications that the underlying misgivings and reluctances about Barkley could force Kefauver to the nomination no matter what the present strategy may be.

In some essential respects Stevenson has been misinterpreted and misunderstood. I also think that he may not quite understand the President. But it is self-evident to me that Stevenson provides the only sure chance of winning the election and of retaining the gains and the carrying out of this Administration's foreign and domestic policies.

Stevenson, it should be noted went through the same personal tortures before he agreed to run for Governor. He literally had to be pushed into it. But once in the race he made a great fight of it and a very good Governor. This is precisely the situation all over again as it concerns the Presidency — only more violently so.

The man Stevenson is burdened with a genuine shyness — but there is no studied aloofness in him. I get the impression that he can't say or do anything to harm the chances of the several active candidates — some of whom are warm friends of his. It really must pain him to contemplate engaging in a contest with any of them.

I therefore earnestly urge that before it is irrevocably too late that you send word to Chairman McKinney that you have decided to remain neutral and to leave it to the Convention to make a free choice — that you will indicate to no one or through no one any personal preference. If you do this by tomorrow Stevenson will be nominated.

David K. Noyes

172

August 11 1952

Dear Dave:

I certainly did appreciate your good letter of the seventh. I was particularly intrigued with the proposal for Ripley's file.

I'll be most happy to see you when you come back and listen to an unprejudiced view of the two Conventions.

Sincerely yours,

Harry Truman

Mr. David M. Noyes
9489 Dayton Way
Beverly Hills, California

November 5, 1952

Dear Dave:

I certainly appreciated your good telegram of
the fourth. We failed to put the proposition over
but the record has been made and I think the
right sort of a record.

Sincerely yours,

Harry Truman

Honorable David M. Noyes
9489 Dayton Way
Beverly Hills, California

Thank you personally for your advice and assistance. I expect to see you soon for more advice and assistance. Bill will be in touch with you.

HST was saddened over the outcome of the election. The Eisenhower campaign, he felt, was an insidious melange of double talk and that the issues were never sharply and clearly defined. He rated Stevenson as being by far the better equipped of the two candidates. Stevenson spoke eloquently, clearly, although at times, over the heads of some of his listeners.

Truman felt, too, that Stevenson understood the vast implications of the American Presidency. He could not understand what it was that made Stevenson falter towards the end of the campaign. Did he feel overwhelmed by the glamour and popularity of the General? Or, did he take the polls too seriously? But, whatever it was, something vital had gone out of Stevenson.

The President could never fathom Stevenson's strategy to detach himself from the incumbent administration. Or, why he felt the need to move the Democratic headquarters out of its traditional place in the capitol to Springfield, Illinois.

Stevenson's second try for the Presidency was even more disappointing than his first. One would have assumed that having faltered and faded toward the closing days of his 1952 campaign, he would have learned how not to surrender to defeatism.

I recall an appearance he made at the Ambassador Hotel in Los Angeles where he addressed an overflow crowd. This was at a critical stage of the campaign. As he was passing my table on the way to the platform, he tapped my shoulder, leaned over and said, "Dave, after this is over, will you come to my room? I need to talk to you."

I sat through one of the most disappointing speeches I had ever heard Stevenson make. From one so richly endowed with the gift of eloquence, his speech fell flat. It lacked substance, cohesion and cadence. It was as though he was impatient to be done with it.

Later, when I joined him in his quarters, I found him sitting in a relaxed posture eating an apple. His staff and well wishers were assembling. Each in turn was patting him on the back, congratulating him on his performance with such observations as, "It was one of your greatest, your best, most powerful..." and other such nonsense. When the last one left, Stevenson rose, shut the door and turned to me and said, "Dave, what did you think of the speech?" It was plain for me to see that he had thrown off the anesthetic of the "well wishers" and that now he was dead serious.

"Adlai, that was the worst speech I ever heard you make. It had no continuity, no theme, and it struck me as a scissors and paste pot job that someone had put together for you. When I compare your performance tonight with your historic speech of acceptance, I am moved to ask what in heaven's name has happened to you?"

He said, "Dave, at this point, I no longer read; I no longer think; I no longer write; and I no longer react. I deliver speeches that are handed to me, and that's all I can do." I realized that this was a punishing ordeal for one so acutely sensitive.

With the campaign over, HST began to cast an eye towards the future destiny of the Party. He felt that after the country had a second taste of the incoming administration, it would be ready in 1960 for the Democrats to take charge once again. In the meantime, it was imperative to keep the Party activated and to keep the public informed.

In that connection, I was delegated by HST to present to Governor Stevenson a way to meet the problem head on:

1. To issue a monthly newsletter to be entitled "The Stevenson Letter," to be limited to eight pages; the content to deal broadly with the basic issues before the nation; the editor to be the commentator Elmer Davis; contributing commentaries to be made by the Speaker of the House, majority leader of the Senate, and chairmen of the important congressional committees; and a comprehensive editorial to be contributed by Adlai Stevenson.

2. To form a national volunteer circulation committee to engage the over 2,000,000 Stevenson volunteers from the previous campaign to secure as many subscribers to "The Stevenson Letter" at $12.00 per year.

3. To provide from these funds quarterly TV and radio time to make reports on the state of the nation; to use a portion of any surplus towards funding the nominee of the Party.

HST communicated with the Governor and arranged for me to meet with him in his Chicago office. I telephoned the Governor on arrival, and he suggested that we have dinner at his club. He seemed interested in learning what he had to propose. I gave him a sketchy outline to which he listened with interest. He put several questions to me which gave me no clue as to his reaction to the concept. We then spoke of other things and reminisced a bit about the campaign. We arranged for another session in his office for the following morning.

That morning session turned out to be a mini-convention. The group consisted of the top echelon of the Democratic National Committee. It seemed they had developed a plan of their own, and what was to have been an evaluation of the outline I brought with me, resulted in a debate as to the relative merits of each plan. Their idea was to issue a publication of their own, modeled after The Reader's Digest, and to be called "The Democratic Digest."

Stevenson sat behind his desk and took no part in the discussion. He was stoically, totally uncommunicative. It soon became apparent there was no further purpose in pursuing a discussion where those assembled could be persuaded to vote against their own project. I reported my experience to HST. He said, "Dave, you were talking to people who were still in a state of shock. Anyone experienced in the fortunes of politics learns to get over their disappointments quickly and to plan for the next day. Take, for instance, a man like Hubert Humphrey. He would be as good as new the next morning." The Democratic Digest, which was adopted in place of the program suggested to Stevenson by HST for the promotion of the Democratic Party, turned out to be a feeble effort, and it suffered an early demise.

HARRY S. TRUMAN
FEDERAL RESERVE BANK BUILDING
KANSAS CITY 6, MISSOURI

March 6, 1953

Dear Dave:

I can't tell you how much I appreciated your good letter of the fourth. It certainly was a pleasure to hear from you and to get your reaction to Governor Stevenson's West Coast speech. I was highly intrigued with your comments on some of the people who are around him.

Mrs. Truman and I expect to leave here on the night of the nineteenth of March and will arrive in San Francisco on the afternoon of the twenty-first. I understand George Killion is having a buffet dinner for us that evening. I don't know where we will stop but I judge it will be at the Fairmont Hotel.

The next morning, the twenty-second, we will board the ship and go to Los Angeles, arriving there, I think on the morning of the twenty-third. The ship stays over in Los Angeles the evening of the twenty-third, at which time I am expecting to have dinner on board ship with Mr. Smith, the editor of the Los Angeles News, Ed Pauley, George Killion and several of our other political friends. I'd be most happy to see you at any one of these places and discuss with you the situation with which I am faced. That doesn't mean I wouldn't be just as pleased to see you in K.C. if you want to make the trip here.

I certainly enjoyed your letter more than I can tell you.

Sincerely yours,

Harry Truman

Honorable David M. Noyes
9489 Dayton Way
Beverly Hills, California

November 24, 1953

Honorable Harry S. Truman
1107 Federal Reserve Bank Building
Kansas City 6, Missouri

Dear Mr. President:

Soon after I returned, I did a bit of sampling of opinion here and in several key parts of the country by telephone. I think it is now safe to conclude that a great many Americans of both parties have undergone a marked change in attitude. They seem to be expressing themselves more openly in this protest against mccarthyism.

What impresses me the most is that so many Democrats for the first time in many months are showing signs of having come to life reunited and reinvigorated in their political faith. On the whole, I found the opinion climate more encouraging than I dared hope. Some of the more zealous of the citizenry have grown quite emotional about you personally, and if New York is any indication of enthusiastic demonstrations - wait till you get out here!

Adlai Stevenson's performance before the Georgia legislature this morning would indicate that he is back in the groove and that he continues to pack a mean rhetorical wallop! Here's hoping for more of the same.

It is clearly evident that your "big Monday" on the networks proved to the world and most of our own people that the voice of free America should not be confused with the voice of a loud, sick minority.

Affectionately,

DMN:mh   DAVID M. NOYES

180

September 27, 1955

Honorable Harry S. Truman
1107 Federal Reserve Bank Building
Kansas City 6, Missouri

Dear Mr. President:

   During my brief stay in Chicago I handed
Mayor Daley his souvenir of your Memoirs. You
never saw a man more flustered and pleased than
he was. He blushed, he grinned, he stammered, and
then managed to say some very nice things about
you and how pleased and honored he was. He is a
good example of a decent and honorable man brought
up in the tradition of practical politics from
the level of the precinct.

   It may interest you to know that one of
the public relations man being consulted by the
Stevenson staff told me that several weeks ago
he had sent in a suggestion about consulting with
a panel of psychiatrists to break down what is
termed as the "father complex", which the public
has developed towards President Eisenhower. These
psychiatrists were to be consulted for advice on
how this "father complex" could be overcome to
Stevenson's benefit. Immediately after this suggestion reached the Stevenson headquarters, the
p.r. man received a reply telling him that they
had been working on this approach since last January and were hoping for a solution. All of this
strikes me as an idea for writing a "who-dunnit",
the title of which would be "The Case of the
Scrambled Eggheads".

   With all best.

       Always,

DMN:mg   DAVID M. NOYES

181

ADLAI E. STEVENSON
231 So. La Salle Street
Chicago

January 10, 1956

Dear Mr. President:

I have just read now the proof sheets of installment 28 of
the Memoirs. I know you will understand my wanting to comment, in
all friendliness, about several of the things you say there about
the 1952 campaign.

Your criticisms are candid, and this permits me to take
pleasure and satisfaction, too, from your kind and indeed charitable
comments regarding our general accomplishments in 1952.

Regarding the "mistakes," I have no thought except to remove
any element of misunderstanding which might in any way have contributed to your feeling about them.

I think you will agree, with respect to my decision to have
a personal friend made Chairman of the National Committee, that if
this was a mistake it was one that the great majority of Presidential
candidates have traditionally made.

I set up my headquarters in Springfield, because I was Governor
of Illinois. It was my capital, and my continuing responsibility
was there throughout the campaign. I could not in good conscience
have done differently about this.

The reference to "the mess in Washington" was, as you very
fairly indicate, an inadvertence. I should perhaps note that this
reference was in a letter, not in an interview. Either in dicta-
tion or in transcription the quotes were left out of my reference
to what the man who had written to me said.

You refer to my "alienating many influential Democratic political leaders at the outset," and thus sacrificing perhaps mil-
lions of votes. I know, of course, that Governor Shivers of Texas
and Governor Kennon of Louisiana were alienated by my position on
tidelands oil. There was a basic principle involved there, one
for which you had stood with vigor. Governor Byrnes of South Caro-
lina and Senator McCarran of Nevada also appear to have opposed my
candidacy. And I am suggesting only that while needless alienation
of Democratic support would seem to me the appropriate subject of
criticism, the loss of support due to a candidate's stand on matters of principle should not.

Of the "poor coordination between Washington and Springfield"
I can only say that I was frankly unaware of it at the time, that
I know from subsequent knowledge that what you say is true, that
I regret it and cannot wholly blame it on what were the inordinate

pressures of the moment.

I am afraid that we do remember differently the conversations and events reflected by your suggestion that "when it seemed to me too late, Stevenson asked me to get into the campaign." We talked about that, as I recall it, only on the occasion of my visit with you in your office in Washington on August 12 when you graciously agreed to make six or seven speeches toward the end of the campaign in major centers in the East and Middle West. You expressed a desire, as I recall, to conclude in St. Louis. You also informed me of a Labor Day commitment, I believe, and a dam dedication together with a speech in California. But your reference to a later and belated request from me to change what I had thought were our arrangements made on August 12 to cover thewhole campaign comes now as a surprise to me. I repeat, though, that I was grateful indeed for all you did.

If you are right that I went "on the defensive in Cleveland and other cities on the question of so-called Communists in Government," I can only say that my words served my intentions very poorly. I could not ignore,but had to correct, the distortions of fact and the even uglier innuendos about my own position on this issue. As I reread these speeches now they seem to me bluntly forthright on the subject of theRepublican campaign smear and slander on the Communist issue. I have spoken in public not once but a score of times my heartfelt belief that you saw this issue clearly and did more than anyone else in the world to fight communism.

Finally, let me say again that while you may be right that if I had accepted"in good faith" your proposal on January 20 (not 30) to run for thenomination I would have received at least three million more votes, I don't see how I could have done it — in goodfaith — even if I had wanted to, because I had already asked the people of Illinois to re-elect me Governor and it was too late to withdraw my petition.

Well! I feel better! And I hope you do too. I know you will realize that this letter is not animated by vexation, but by the hope that giving you my understanding of these things may diminish a little your own feeling about them.

I know there were mistakes. I know, too, that you will share with me the consolation I got the other day from an advertisement headline: "Everybody Has 20-20 Hindsight."

You know, from what I have already said elsewhere, about my admiration for your extraordinary workmanship in compiling thesememoirs. That feeling is unchanged.

Respectfully yours,

/s/ Adlai E. Stevenson

PS I assume you have seen the enclosed admirable review from the London Times Literary Supplement.

January 13, 1956

Dear Dave:

I certainly appreciated your letter of the twelfth concerning Time and Life and the statements of MacArthur and Dulles. I don't think we should take any notice of Mr. Dulles for the reason that he was only following orders in anything he did while working for Dean Acheson.

I am enclosing a copy of a letter from Adlai which I think you will find interesting. I haven't answered it. I may see him in Minnesota tomorrow night, and if I do, I know he will discuss the situation with me. I'll probably write you about it after I have talked to him. The letter isn't so bad.

Sincerely yours,

Harry Truman

Hon. David M. Noyes
9489 Dayton Way
Beverly Hills, California

Enc.

DAVID M. NOYES
9489 DAYTON WAY
BEVERLY HILLS, CALIFORNIA

April 17, 1956

Honorable Harry S. Truman
1107 Federal Reserve Bank Building
Kansas City 6, Missouri

Dear Mr. President:

A message from Stevenson informs me that he will use a substantial portion of the foreign policy speech I read to you. But I fear that he will obscure much of the meaning with rhetorical embellishments.

Upon further reflection it seems to me that the Governor is encumbered with psychological difficulties which may add up to a personality defect. He does not appear to be gifted with the instinct of sharp political focus, nor the sense of political trends.

I find it difficult to account for the contrast between his high intelligence and his inability to deal with the obvious.

There also seems to be a question of capacity for sound judgment, and the ability to make decisions and then resolutely carry them out. You know better than anyone how important these characteristics are to the conduct of the American Presidency.

These are some of the questions that remain to be resolved as I think back on my recent talks with Stevenson. There is even less to comfort one in contemplating the qualifications of all other current aspirants.

With all best.

Always,

HARRY S. TRUMAN
FEDERAL RESERVE BANK BUILDING
KANSAS CITY 6, MISSOURI

April 26, 1956

Dear Dave:— Your letter was most intriguing— a mild statecat.

The analysis of the Governor is certainly a correct one. What a hell of a situation to develop when a man has education par excellence, background equal to the commanding general of the Light Brigade, experience as an administrator and a foreign affairs background. All that is lacking is a coordination of these qualifications with plain old Missouri horse sense and a love and sympathy with people from the gutter to the mansion.

God, what an opportunity he had! Hope you'll forgive me for this. Maybe we'd better take the Baptist view of a Presbyterian. "What is to be will be whether it happens or not."

I've a great letter from Cominsky on the comming campaign and one from Max Ascoli which I'll show you when you are this way.

I signed those books for you and put a note in the one for your mother and sister with some good advice about their son and brother.

My best to your "Boss" + the boy.

Sincerely

Harry Truman

August 27, 1956

Dear Dave:

I have had several thousand letters on the Chicago convention, and there are probably another thousand outside this morning.

I have read every one, and they run 3 or 4 to 1 in my favor. I hope we have stirred up the animals to the extent that we can put the ticket over this fall.

Mrs. Truman and I were very happy to receive the telegram from your mother. We sincerely hope that she is getting along all right. The luncheon with Dr. Bundesen was one of the highlights of my trip to Chicago. I enjoyed myself very much.

I would like to hear from you on the reaction in California.

Sincerely yours,

Harry Truman

Hon. David M. Noyes
9489 Dayton Way
Beverly Hills, California

November 2, 1956

C
O
P
Y

Dear Mr. President:

You were right as usual. I found this quotation:

"... FINDS TONGUES IN TREES,
    BOOKS IN THE RUNNING BROOKS,
  SERMONS IN STONES,
    AND GOOD IN EVERYTHING".

It is in Shakespeare's "As You Like It", Act 2, Scene 1, Line 2. I am glad I knew from experience not to bet you.

It was wonderful to see you again. Please remember me warmly to Mrs. Truman.

Always,

DMN:MG   DAVID M. NOYES

Honorable Harry S. Truman
1107 Federal Reserve Bank Bldg.
Kansas City 6, Missouri

189

November 6, 1956

Dear Dave:

Thank you very much for your note of the 2nd.

I had found the quotation in "As You Like It,"
and you'd never guess how I came to find it. Mrs.
Truman told me; she remembers it on the old Shubert
curtain. The whole paragraph is good, and when we quote
it, I believe we should use it in its entirety.

I hope you voted this morning, but I feel that
our votes won't count for much this time. And this is
the first election in which I've been a pessimist.

Sincerely yours,

Harry Truman

Hon, David M. Noyes
9489 Dayton Way
Beverly Hills, California

CHAPTER 12

JFK AND TRUMAN

For HST, the presidential election year of 1960 could not have arrived any too soon. For eight years he had witnessed this nation being governed by a Presidency which had functioned in almost direct contravention to the two previous administrations. The policies and the many historic decisions of the Truman administration had advanced the United States to a position of leadership in the free world, and Truman was concerned that the continuity of that leadership be maintained. He felt strongly that throughout the eight years of the Eisenhower administration the nation had been ministered by a "caretaker government."

In the highly sensitive area of foreign policy, President Eisenhower delegated and for all practical purposes, relegated, power to his brash Secretary of State, John Foster Dulles. Dulles proceeded to frighten friend and foe alike by his doctrine of "Brinkmanship."

Dulles was well known to Truman. He had used Dulles in his administration, but never to originate foreign policy. His duties were confined to special assignments, for which he was carefully and specifically briefed and instructed.

President Truman had hoped that President Eisenhower would associate himself with a man of experience in foreign affairs and a sense of history for America's new role in charting a course for a world at peace. Truman had good reason to feel uneasy about Dulles' appointment and policies. The price we had to pay for the malfunction of the State Department was the irreparable damage perpetrated by the capricious action in abandoning the Aswan Dam project to the Russians, thereby providing them with a strong foothold in the Middle East, plus a base of operations from which to cause all kinds of mischief. The intervention into the British, French, Israeli joint operation in repossession of the Suez Canal had sown the seeds of the tragedies that were soon to follow.

In 1960, Truman set his hopes for the world's future on the restoration of the White House to Democratic leadership. He felt that Stevenson had been drained through two difficult campaigns and could not be regarded as a viable candidate. However, he felt the prospects for the Democratic Party were excellent, but that the party needed to exercise great care in choosing the most qualified and also the most electable candidate.

He had known Hubert Humphrey from their Senate days and regarded him as the best evolved candidate. Humphrey had pioneered in many heroic congressional decisions and had an extraordinary grasp of the intricacies of our government. Another senator whom Truman regarded as a worthy presidential candidate was Lyndon B. Johnson, who was a protégé of Speaker of the House Sam Rayburn. There were others in the offing whose candidacies were yet to mature. Time and convention would tell.

The unexpected and unforeseen declaration by John Fitzgerald Kennedy that he would seek the Presidency in 1960, was a jolt to Truman's hopes. From the very outset of Kennedy's announcement, the President let it be known that JFK's candidacy was unacceptable to him. Truman felt there was nothing in his record in the U. S. Senate which was distinguished, and even more troublesome was the fact that Senator Kennedy was not identified with any major issues of the times. President Truman believed that John F. Kennedy's candidacy was the product of his father's long standing ambition for his son.

As the campaign unfolded, a spirited battle was waged between Humphrey and Kennedy in state primary elections. In the State of West Virginia, the advance work by the Kennedy forces succeeded in capturing enough counties to assure Humphrey's defeat. This was a critical test of strength and a mortal blow to Humphrey's national chances. The outcome in West Virginia was expected to favor Humphrey, but an adroit maneuver by the Kennedy advance men who capitalized upon the curious political structure of West Virginia politics, (in which party control is vested in the county sheriffs), engineered a turnabout. From that time on, Kennedy's candidacy developed a momentum which disarmed and discouraged all other aspirants and pushed them into the background.

President Truman responded to the Kennedy steamroller by issuing a public statement which postulated the all important question of Kennedy's inexperience and youth: "Senator Kennedy, are you sure you are ready for the country, and that the country is ready for you?" At the same time he publicly posed this question, Truman announced that he could not attend the Democratic Convention because he felt that the convention had been deprived of means and methods by which it was truly representative of the Democratic Party. Harry Truman was a true traditionalist, and this decision was a bitter pill for him to swallow. Those of us who were in close association with him knew and understood how soul wrenching and agonizing it was for him not to be there with his party.

Independence, Missouri

As you already know I have resigned as a delegate from Missouri to the Democratic National Convention. I did this because I have no desire whatever to be a party to proceedings that are taking on the aspects of a pre-arranged affair.

A Convention which is controlled in advance by one group, and its candidate, leaves the delegates no opportunity for a democratic choice and reduces the convention to a mockery.

I have always believed that the Democratic Party should stand for an open convention and should resist any bandwagon that thwarts and stifles the free and deliberative process of this great instrument of democracy. And the Democratic Party must never be allowed to become a party of privilege where men of modest means, or no means at all, cannot rise to service in the nation.

I am speaking up at this time because I would hope that many of the delegates, who have been stampeded or pressured into pre-convention commitments against their better judgments—and I know at firsthand of such instances—will have a chance to exercise further judgment.

There is yet time, before the convention opens July 11, for delegates to reflect on their individual responsibilities to the party and to the nation. For this is a time of great difficulty in the world and we cannot afford to be swayed by personal likes or dislikes. And we must be careful not to permit ourselves to be moved by personal prejudices or religious bigotry.

The future usefulness of the party, and the restoration of direction and leadership to the nation, are of such paramount importance that I am impelled to disregard the pleadings of some of my friends to remain silent about the situation that has developed. They have urged me not to do anything to upset or offend anyone by speaking up now.

But I could not remain silent because I think it would be tragic if the Convention were to allow any one clique to ride herd over it. To let this happen could very well frustrate the hopes and desire of the American people to return a Democrat to the White House.

This is the first National Democratic Convention I shall miss since I became United States Senator in Nineteen Hundred and Thirty-four. And it is a matter of great regret and deep emotion for me to stay away from the proceedings of my party, which has honored me so greatly, and has always been so kind and generous to me personally. But the times are such that the future success of the party, and the restoration of leadership to the nation, compel me to forego personal consideration to do whatever I can to alert the Los Angeles convention.

I want to make it clear that my disappointment at the manner in which some of the backers of Senator John F. Kennedy have acted, involves in no way, in my own mind the person or qualifications of the Senator himself. I think, to a great extent, Senator Kennedy is a victim of circumstances brought on by some of his over zealous backers which is unfortunate and unfair to him.

Senator Kennedy has demonstrated ability, capacity and energy to play an important and continuing role in the party and the government. I have always liked him personally and I still do-and because of this feeling, I would want to say to him at this time: "Senator, are you certain that you are quite ready for the country, or that the country is ready for you in the role of President in January of Nineteen Hundred and Sixty-One. I have no doubt about the political heights to which you are destined to rise. But I am deeply concerned and troubled about the situation we are up against in the world now and in the immediate future. That is why I would hope that someone with the greatest possible maturity and experience would be available at this time. May I urge you to be patient? You will recall that I suggested to you at our meeting in Independence that all personal ambitions be put aside and that we all join forces to seek out such a man, who could unite us in purpose and action."

And I would say to the delegates that the Democrats must not make the mistake of freezing out men who by their public service and record have proved themselves worthy of fair consideration by an unbound convention. I feel strongly that the Democratic convention owes it to the people to arrive at its choice after due deliberation no matter how long it takes.

The position of Vice President was also of great concern to Truman. Sam Rayburn and Lyndon Johnson had been in constant communication with Harry Truman in the days before the convention, but events moved so quickly that they were unable to get word to Independence before the public announcement that LBJ had accepted a draft by Kennedy for the second spot. However, the day after the convention, LBJ rushed to Kansas City to give a personal account and explanation to Truman.

This meeting took place in a suite at the Muehlebach Hotel. I was working on a manuscript in an adjacent room and could hear the murmur of two familiar voices. Suddenly, the voices grew loud and kept increasing in volume and pitch. This was must unusual for HST. On impulse, I walked over and opened the door. Lyndon Johnson stood with arms outstretched pleading and saying, "If you don't help me in Texas, I cannot carry the state."

To keep the record straight, there was nothing personal in Truman's opposition to John Kennedy. As a matter of fact, he always liked JFK as a person. Mr. Truman, a lifetime observer of the United States Senate and a former member, instinctively felt that Kennedy needed some more seasoning, some more give and take at other levels and there were others in the picture. He was much more concerned however with the cabal around Kennedy, most of whom were hirelings of Joe Kennedy and reluctantly, he proposed some remarks for the upcoming convention.

With the nomination of Senator John F. Kennedy for President and Senator Lyndon B. Johnson for Vice President, the Democratic Party must now close ranks and go to work.

The restoration of Democratic leadership and direction to the nation is essential in the face of the world situation.

No differences among us, whatever they may be, can be important enough to impair our unity at a time when the security and the survival of this nation and of the free world are in jeopardy.

And let us be sure that in the coming campaign we do not say or do anything that would give Communist Russia or Red China reason to doubt the determination of all or people, of whatever political party, to resist to the utmost encroachment by them either in the Western Hemisphere or elsewhere in the free world.

If we are to succeed in our bid for leadership we must wage a vigorous and inspiring campaign to bring all the facts to the American people.

To that end I pledge my personal services in any way that I may be asked by the party.

* * * * * * * * *

Ultimately, Mr. Truman did embark upon an arduous and active schedule campaigning for the Kennedy/Johnson ticket. Word reached him in Dallas that the Baptist ministers, as a body, passed a resolution to oppose Kennedy for the Presidency. Truman, (a Baptist in his own right), appeared before this group. Never one to mince words, he went right to the point, "If you have opposed to the candidacy of Kennedy because you regard him as not being sufficiently fit to undertake that high office, that is your privilege. But, if you are opposed to him because of his Catholicism, then you will go to hell."

This public rebuke to religious prejudice hit a sensitive nerve in many areas—as it was meant to do. The issue covered a key tenet in our democracy and had to be met head on. It brought a shower of abuse as well as some praise, but HST had made his point. He often said to me that there were times he felt it was necessary to use strong or harsh words because, "I needed to shock the people out of their apathy." He believed that the public needed to be prodded in order to keep them aware of what their government was doing. To achieve that, he sometimes used unorthodox methods. This practice earned him the accolade "the master of calculated indiscretion."

Soon after his nomination, Kennedy telephoned Truman to arrange a meeting which would be followed by a joint press conference. Kennedy realized that he needed Truman's help in resolving many of the problems of the coming presidential campaign. Kennedy came to Independence, accompanied by Senator Henry Jackson from the State of Washington who was the newly appointed chairman of the Democratic Committee. The meeting was held in the auditorium of the Truman Library and attracted broad coverage from all the media.

At the outset, there were a number of exploratory questions of current interest to which Kennedy responded with ease. These inquiries were followed by questions of major significance dealing with issues such as peace, economy, problems with the Communist world and the Middle East. These questions were directed not to JFK but to President Truman, who neatly folded and redirected them to Kennedy with the comment, "The Senator is perfectly able to respond on his own." Unhappily, on questions of such scope Kennedy was not prepared to respond with assurance and authority. From where I sat, he seemed to be quite uncomfortable and clearly ill at ease. (In retrospect, this conference was in sharp contrast to the stellar performances he exhibited after he became the President.)

After the interview, Truman was visibly agitated, and on the way back to his office he gripped my arm saying, "Dave, what are we going to do? I wanted him to make the most of the opportunity; I expected him to come up with the right answers. Dave, he didn't do it. He didn't do it. Dave, he didn't know! What are we going to do?" Truman was in the depths of disappointment and discouragement.

Bill Hillman and I were on the way to join HST and Kennedy and other guests for lunch when I recalled the close relationship between Bill and the Kennedy family. So I asked Bill to find out what had gone wrong at the press conference which had made the candidate so ill at ease and upset President Truman so much. Bill immediately strode over to Kennedy and questioned, "Jack, what happened to you? This was one test you could not afford to fail, but you blew it!"

Pointing a finger at Harry Truman, Kennedy replied, "That man scares me. That man really scares me!"

After the election and campaign were behind them, the two men, Kennedy and Truman, grew closer together. An historic illustration of this congruence occurred when Kennedy returned from Vienna after his nerve shattering encounter with Khrushchev. Immediately upon landing on American soil, Kennedy rushed to a telephone and briefed President Truman on his meeting with Khrushchev. He closed the phone call with the following words, "Mr. President, he's an even bigger S.O.B. than you ever thought he was!"

Kennedy never forgot the importance of Truman's contribution to his election. On the night of his victory, Kennedy went into seclusion to contemplate the grave responsibilities he was about to assume. His first call went to President Truman to whom he expressed his gratitude for making the outcome possible. He later inscribed his portrait to President Truman with this quote, "To the man who put me in the White House."

Shortly after Kennedy felt firmly established in the Presidency, he initiated the practice of informing HST about trends and developments in international affairs. Periodically, Truman responded to a particular issue raised by a Kennedy letter. HST was much concerned by Kennedy's difficulties with Congress, and would send him a commendatory letter whenever he felt Kennedy took a strong stance upon an important piece of legislation. In one such letter he wrote, "You have now assumed the Presidency in total and in your own right. No President worthy of the office ever accomplishes very much when he prefers a harmonious relationship with Congress."

The whole world and its leaders were concerned about nuclear pollution in the atmosphere as a result of nuclear tests. President Kennedy undertook to solve this problem by trying to reach a joint agreement with Russia to confine all nuclear tests to underground facilities. He sent a declaration to Moscow to attempt to negotiate such an agreement. It was a difficult undertaking, for the Russians suspected that any such proposal from the West was designed to weaken their military capacity.

President Kennedy kept Truman fully advised of all the negotiations, (both progress and obstacles), and when after months of laborious and hairsplitting arguments by both sides, a treaty was finally hammered out, a copy was immediately dispatched to Truman asking for his comments and criticisms. HST read and studied the treaty with meticulous care. He felt and noted that certain provisions and passages needed further clarification. Kennedy agreed with Truman's points and comments, and the treaty went back for revision. This revised version was also submitted to HST, and he found it more acceptable. He expressed the hope that by the first effort to curb a nuclear threat to the world, more efforts would continue to remove for all time the threat of a nuclear holocaust.

The accompanying letters concerning the treaty sent by President Kennedy to HST were obviously typed by Kennedy himself. They each had the meticulous style of presidential letters; words were crossed out, typos were Xed out, not the work of a skilled White House secretary. President Kennedy wanted to preserve total privacy between himself and Truman.

An interesting side to Kennedy's nature was related to me by the Director General, Dr. Hertzog, of the Prime Minister's Office of Israel, when I was President Truman's representative in connection with the Harry S. Truman International Center for the Advancement of Peace. Dr. Hertzog wanted to share with me a page out of his experiences with President Kennedy.

Dr. Hertzog and Kennedy became good friends when Kennedy was a U. S. Senator. Shortly after Kennedy's election, Dr. Hertzog was assigned to Canada as Ambassador from Israel. In this post, he found himself alone and neglected in the company of the Diplomatic Corps. As President, Kennedy traveled to Canada to foster better understanding and closer cooperation between the two countries. During a formal reception honoring President Kennedy, and to which the whole Diplomatic Corps had been invited, Dr. Hertzog found himself in his usual spot: "The end of the line, almost out of sight." Kennedy spotted Hertzog at the end of the line as he entered the room. He headed right to his old friend and embraced him. Hertzog laughingly told me, "At that moment, I stood ten feet tall, and from that day on, I was a welcome member, at least in GOOD standing, if not HIGH standing, of the Diplomatic Corps in Canada."

When I related that story to Truman, he observed dryly that, "Kennedy was rising to the call of the Presidency at a steady pace."

CHAPTER 13

DECISION NOT TO RUN

In discussing with President Truman the consequences of his decisions not to stand for re-election in 1952, he made the following observations:

"I made a serious mistake when I decided not to run again in 1952. I thought that the people then wanted a change and I also had some feelings about a third term. It is true that I was specifically exempted from the Constitutional Amendment limiting a President to two terms and that I had only one term on my own and served out the unexpired Roosevelt term; but for practical purposes it could be considered that I had served two terms.

In reflecting on that decision these thoughts occurred to me.

If I had run in 1952, it is reasonably certain that General Eisenhower would not have declared himself.

Inevitably, the Republican nominee would have been Senator Robert Taft.

And, I think it is fair to assume that in a choice between Taft and me, the voters would have acted in '52 as they had in '48.

And, as I look back on the situation, I feel that the shape of things might have turned out differently if I had continued in order to 'finish the job.'

It seems clear to me now that some of the things that had befallen us might have been prevented. Here are some examples of some of the defeats we had sustained:

1. Precarious truce in Korea in place of a permanent settlement.
2. Our action in abandoning Suez and forcing its surrender to Nasser. This was a major tragedy and a grave blunder. It produced another spot on the globe where a war potential was created.
3. The misjudgment of the Cuban revolution and our failure to deal with it realistically.
4. The Little Rock incident with Faubus, et. al. The incident could have been prevented. Instead, it was one of the most unfortunate inflammatory outbreaks, which left a permanent scar on the nation.
5. The delay in pushing for civil rights following the Supreme Court decision on school desegregation. The consequences of the Administration's weakness in supporting this decision led to the outbreaks in the North as well as in South.
6. The gradual dissipation of American prestige abroad and the decline of our leadership is resulting in some dangerous developments and disunity among the allies.
7. The meetings in Geneva between General Eisenhower and Krushchev and Bulganin, did not advance the cause of peace. It only served to intensify the Cold War and provide an opportunity for these two successors to Stalin to gain world recognition.
8. The handling of the U-2 incident and the humiliating experience of our President in his meeting with Khrushchev in Paris, provided

the enemies of the West with another opportunity to make capital at our expense.

9. The decline of the United Nations as a moral force in the world councils is clearly related to the loss of leadership of the United States.

10. The behavior of Charles DeGaulle and his hostility towards the United States can be disassociated from the series of strategic blunders we have made in conducting our foreign policy.'"

President Truman then went on to discuss the present financial predicament of the United Nations and thought that it was advisable to let the crisis run its course. That if some of the members who are now balking would begin to realize that we are no longer to be expected to assume the obligations of other members they will then perhaps find ways to pay up.

He further delved into the language of diplomacy and thought that it was designed not to inform as to obscure. He referred to the State Department people to compose the State Department statements as the "fuzzy boys." He further said that these were calculated to be imprecise and represent a habit of long standing in all chanceries.

What he went out to say, everything depends on what a President in office says and how he says it, so as to make it clear to the rest of the world on what is in our minds and what is our purpose as a nation. This, only a President can do with the finality of the authority that is vested in him. Only he can tell our friends and foes alike what is in our minds and what we intend to do about it.

CHAPTER 14

FINAL YEARS

HST & TV

HST knew that, in the long perspective of time, history would attend to the ultimate record of his administration. But, between the day of judgment and the present, there would be a twilight zone of assumptions, speculations, opinions, and interpretations of contemporary writers who would base their conclusions on second and third hand sources. Eager historians might presume what a President had in mind without ever having had access to that mind.

Anticipating this, HST decided to leave a first-hand account of his administration. His two-volume "Memoirs" came out in 1956, followed four years later (1960) by "Mr. Citizen," a personal reflection on his homecoming. Concurrently he wrote a syndicated monthly commentary on foreign policy (North American Newspaper Alliance).

With the books wrapped up, Bill Hillman and I introduced to Truman the idea of making a television series to encompass the major decisions and events of his White House years. We pointed out to him that it was a major loss to history, to the American people, and indeed to the world, that FDR did not live to do a TV series for himself. He had had so much to tell that would now never see the light of day.

Truman knew that such an undertaking would be a taxing and punishing experience. He was 77 years old and had recently undergone major surgery. Under these circumstances, it would have been prudent for him to spare himself, but he decided to go through with it, realizing that it would be a race against time. In those years he often remarked to me that he was being hotly pursued by a determined woman whom he referred to as "Anno Domini." He recalled that Churchill was prevented by the "oncoming years" from taking part himself in the TV series recording his own historic service. In his case, an actor stood in for him.

Bill and I asked Charles Glett, a top executive in motion pictures and television, to help us out with the networks. Glett had been in charge of the Pacific coast operations of CBS, and later a Vice President of National General Theaters. He was impressed with the personality as well as the person of the President and saw the possibility of making a highly successful and instructive series with HST as its star.

During 1960 and 1961, we had innumerable sessions with the networks, but to no avail. It was evident that they neither understood nor sensed the historic importance of such a series, and why such a series needed to be recorded while HST was still able to do it! One network indicated a possible interest if they could have a deciding voice in the content as well as in the treatment. Another came up with a proposal to make one episode to circulate among potential sponsors. Herewith some correspondence with NBC-TV illustrates the thinking of the decision makers of the networks.

Having failed to interest the networks, Truman now asked us to look into other possibilities for producing a series. Of course, we knew that doing it independently of a network would entail hardships involving studio facilities, funding, personnel, and many other things that a network was organized to provide. But, having no choice, we proceeded to try it the hard way.

Paramount Pictures had just become associated with the David Susskind TV producing organization. We were in New York City at that time in connection with the projected publication of a Truman work entitled "The History of the American Presidency." We set up an appointment with Barney Balaban, head of Paramount, to discuss the possibility of producing the series through the Susskind organization. The meeting took place in the President's suite at the Carlyle Hotel. It was forthright and businesslike, and in short order, we arrived at an agreement providing for the production of a minimum of twelve one-hour episodes.

Truman now had renewed hope that at long last the recording of the major events of his Administration seemed assured. However, he admonished us that when the contractual details were worked out, to make sure that we would retain full control over the content so that there would be no distortion of the facts.

As the production series got underway, it soon became evident that the Susskind people were more interested in dramatization than in the drama that was inherent in the subject matter itself. Merle Miller and others on the Susskind staff conducted endless hours of interviews with friends, relatives, acquaintances and Truman himself that always seemed to skirt the main issues of the Truman Administration. Their primary objective appeared to be manner rather than matter, and out of months of preparation and filming, they managed to put together two deplorably unimpressive episodes. It then came out that their intention was not to produce the whole series, but only these two episodes for selling purposes.

Production was halted, and we were informed that they were unable to proceed.

August 14, 1961

Dear Dave:

I appreciated most highly your letter of the 8th,
with the copy of the letter to David Susskind
enclosed. We have quite a job before us and I
am sincerely hoping that it will work out to the
satisfaction of all concerned.

The program which is outlined in the book that
you gave me seems to me to cover the situation
very well but what I am most interested in is,
will people listen to it?

I don't know whether I can put it over or not but
I will try my best.

Sincerely yours,

Harry Truman

Honorable David M. Noyes
567 Comstock Avenue
Los Angeles 24, California

December 27, 1962

Dear Mr. Sarnoff:

Mr. Truman has shared with me his recent exchanges with you. It would appear that Mr. Truman had assumed you were aware that in December of 1960 an approach was made to NBC to negotiate the production of the Truman series by NBC and that this was rejected in a letter from Mr. Robert E. Kintner from which we quote:

"I do not believe the situation has changed regarding a regular series built around President Truman. We have been developing in PROJECT 20 one or two special shows and in one of these we do propose to try to interest President Truman. We have just finished a show with former President Hoover on the life of President Wilson and we are thinking of asking President Truman to comment on the life of President Jackson. I think there already have been discussions with President Truman about this.

At the present time we have so many public affairs projects up for 1961 that I would doubt we would have the opportunity to utilize President Truman properly except perhaps in a special."

One more thing. It was proposed by this intermediary that a personal meeting between the writer and the National Broadcasting Company might prove useful. But we were informed that NBC preferred not to have such a meeting.

These are the facts as we understand them - and as we related them to President Truman.   With all good wishes.

Yours sincerely,

Mr. Robert Sarnoff
Chairman of the Board
National Broadcasting Company
RCA Building, Radio City
New York 20, New York

It is a nice way to tell him to go to hell. I'd use plainer language and will when the opportunity offers! HST

213

Since we were given to understand from the very outset that we had a firm commitment for the total series, I telegraphed Mr. Balaban, informing him of Susskind's failure to perform. In response to my message, Mr. Balaban replied that Paramount only had a 50% interest in the Susskind Productions, but it was a separate corporation and they had no responsibility for it.

October 16, 1961

Dear Mr. Balaban:

The people assigned to the recording and filming
of "Time for Decision" have been working here
for over a week, and I am pleased at the way they
have gone about it and at what is being accomplished.

I hope that the entire series will be produced in
that spirit and that this critical period in our history
will be interestingly and faithfully put together, not
only for our own times but for the generations that
will follow.

Sincerely yours,

HARRY S. TRUMAN

Mr. Barney Balaban
President
Paramount Pictures Corporation
1501 Broadway
New York, New York

COPY

PARAMOUNT INTERNATIONAL FILMS, Inc.

1501 Broadway
New York 36, N. Y.

Office of The President

October 26, 1961

Mr. Harry S. Truman
Independence
Missouri

Dear Mr. President:

I was most pleased to receive your letter of
October 16th relating to "Time for Decision,"
and to be informed that the dedicated task of
preserving your eight very momentous years
in world history is proceeding so smoothly.

On being shown your letter, David Susskind
expressed deep pleasure and again affirmed both the
pride that he has in this task, and our determination to give to posterity the most faithful record of
your two terms as president of the United States,
and the vital and fruitful impact they had on Mankind.

Again, let me express the pride that Talent Associates-
Paramount Limited have in this undertaking.

Sincerely yours,

S/ Barney Balaban
Barney Balaban,

COPY

cc x - David M. Noyes
William Hillman

216

November 20, 1961

Mr. Barney Balaban
Paramount Pictures Corporation   PERSONAL AND CONFIDENTIAL
Paramount Building
New York, New York

PRODUCTION OF THE PRESIDENT TRUMAN SERIES "TIME FOR DECISION" HAS
BEEN ABRUPTLY SUSPENDED. SUSSKIND NOW INFORMS US THAT TALENT
ASSOCIATES-PARAMOUNT LTD. WOULD BE "BANKRUPTED" IF ITS COMMITMENT
TO PRODUCE THE TRUMAN SERIES WERE TO BE FULFILLED AND THAT PARAMOUNT
FUNDS ARE NOT AVAILABLE TO PRODUCE THE SERIES. THIS COMES AS A
SHOCKING DEVELOPMENT IN VIEW OF THE UNCONDITIONAL ASSURANCES MADE
IN NEW YORK CITY LAST JUNE TO PRESIDENT TRUMAN PERSONALLY AS WELL
AS AT THE PRESS CONFERENCE ADDRESSED BY BOTH YOU AND THE PRESIDENT.
WE SINCERELY HOPE YOU WILL TAKE WHATEVER STEPS ARE NECESSARY
TO HASTEN COMPLETION OF THIS HISTORIC PROJECT. SINCEREST PERSONAL
REGARDS.

cc: Hon. Harry S. Truman   David M. Noyes
    Harold H. Stern, Esq.   567 Comstock Avenue .
                               Los Angeles

217

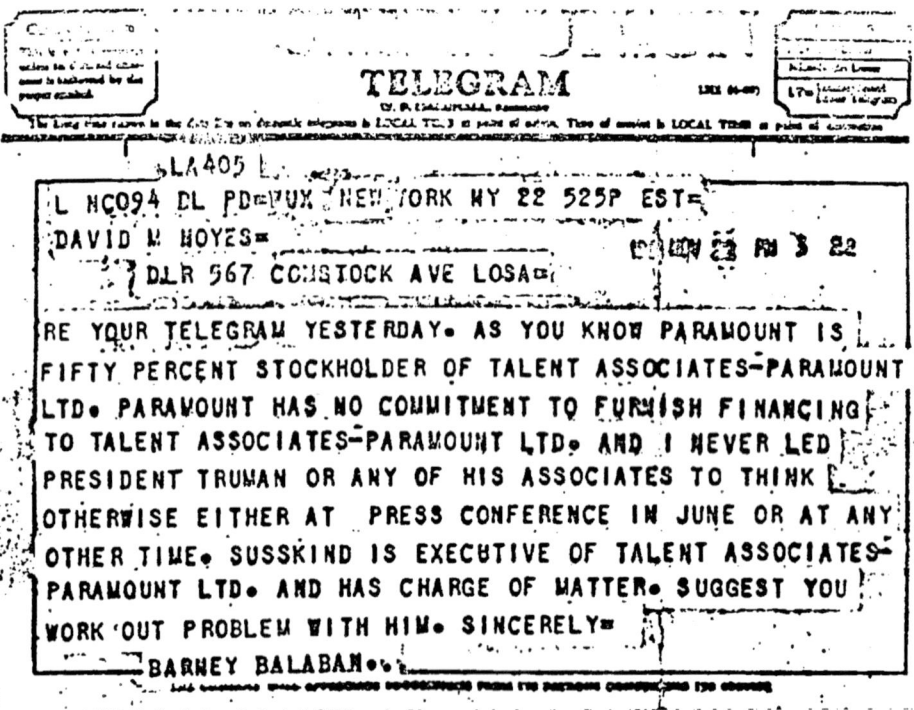

This was a shocking development, and the President was moved to ask, "What manner of people are these?"

HST's disappointment and displeasure in his experience with Susskind's attempt to produce his TV series was further exacerbated by the breach of a binding commitment not to use any of the material for the private or personal gain of any members of Susskind's organization. In 1963, shortly after the termination of the contract with Susskind, one of the writers assigned to the contract made a brazen attempt to have a story of his published in the *Saturday Evening Post* which sensationalized and exploited his very brief contact with the President. The content was so patently raw and vulgar that the editor of the *Post* was constrained to seek clearance for the article from HST.

218

Needless to say, these distortions and perversions outraged Truman, and he instruction his attorney, Harold Fendler, to prohibit publication in the strongest possible terms. The article was never published. Herewith the correspondence which brought that about.

April 15.

Dear Mr. President,

I am enclosing a copy of a piece I have written concerning some of our conversations and experiences while working on the television programs. The piece has now been sold to The Saturday Evening Post. I do hope that you will like it.

Do please give my best regards to Mrs. Truman and to Miss Conway. I am told that my friend Joe McCarthy is now in Independence writing a piece about you for Holiday. If you would be so kind, please give him my best.

I hope one day soon to see you again,

Respectfully,

April 25, 1963

The Editor

Saturday Evening Post

Curtis Publishing Company

609 Fifth Avenue

New York, New York

We have just sent the following telegram to Merle Miller in reference to an article entitled "Truman" which he claims to have sold to the *Saturday Evening Post*:

> "Please be advised that your article entitled 'Truman' sold to the Saturday Evening Post is false and defamatory in many respects and completely unauthorized by President Truman who is shocked and outraged by it and will take all measures necessary to prevent publication."

President Truman feels that the article is not only highly injurious to him but is contrary to the public interest and that your own sense of public responsibility will impel you to comply with this request not to publish the article or any portion thereof. Will you kindly advise the undersigned immediately as to your intentions so that we may notify President Truman.

Fendler, Gershon & Warner

By Harold A. Fendler

Attorneys for President Harry S. Truman

9465 Wilshire Boulevard

Beverly Hills, California

FENDLER, GERSHON & WARNER

WILSHIRE-BEVERLY CENTRE BUILDING

9465 WILSHIRE BOULEVARD

BEVERLY HILLS, CALIFORNIA

HAROLD A. FENDLER
HARRY L. GERSHON
GLENN WARNER
MIRIAM O. FENDLER
DOUGLAS FENDLER
GARY COOPER

TELEPHONES
BRadshaw 2-216
CRestview 1-2156
CABLE ADDRESS "FENWEB"

April 26, 1963

Mr. David M. Noyes
567 Comstock Avenue
Los Angeles 24, California

Dear Dave:

Enclosed are copies of the telegrams sent to Merle Miller and the Saturday Evening Post, as well as the letters to President Truman and Harold Stern, which are self-explanatory.

It is imperative that Charles Glett and President Truman sign all of the necessary documents in connection with HST Associates, and that the President, Mr. McFarland, you and I, sign all the necessary papers with reference to Independence Productions. Before you leave for Independence, please plan on having Glett and McFarland sign all the documents here, and then you can personally attend to getting President Truman's signature in Independence.

With best personal regards,

Sincerely,

HAROLD A. FENDLER

HAF:SK
Enc.

Also enclosed is the copy of telegram from Clay Blair Jr.

223

LAW OFFICES

FENDLER, GERSHON & WARNER

WILSHIRE-BEVERLY CENTRE BUILDING

9465 WILSHIRE BOULEVARD

BEVERLY HILLS, CALIFORNIA

TELEPHONES
BRADSHAW 2 2 6
CRESTVIEW 1 2 56

CABLE ADDRESS "FENWEB"

April 26, 1963

Honorable Harry S. Truman
Truman Library
Independence, Missouri

Dear Mr. President:

   I am enclosing copies of the telegrams composed by David Noyes and myself, which were dispatched yesterday to Merle Miller and to the editor of the Saturday Evening Post. I have just received a telegraphic reply from Clay Blair, Jr., editor of the Post, who states that Miller's article will not be published under any circumstances without your approval. I read the telegram to Dave over the telephone, and I am enclosing a copy of it for your file.

   Yesterday, I spoke to Harold Stern by telephone, and he agreed to contact David Susskind immediately to see what pressure could be exerted on Miller to withdraw the article. I also wrote Stern, as per copy of letter enclosed, because I want it to be a matter of record that Susskind and Talent Associates have a major responsibility for anything Miller has done or may do in the future.

   I trust we will have better luck in our new dealings with Screen Gems, and that your confidences and forthrightness will be more fully respected. In this connection, I think all legal obstacles have been overcome. I have prepared all necessary papers to dissolve HST Associates, Inc. and to implement the new contract with Independence Productions.

   With best personal regards, I remain

       Respectfully yours,

       HAROLD A. FENDLER

HAF:SK
Enc.
Air Mail
cc: Mr. David M. Noyes

No further effort to publish this material was attempted during the period from 1963 throughout the lifetime of HST. Two years after his death, however, the article discredited by Truman had been blown up into a book, much of which drew on tapes and research material to which the author was never privileged, material which had been acquired from Susskind/Talent Associates for a substantial sum by Screen Gems, who did produce the entire series of 26 episodes entitled "Decision."

It should be noted that Screen Gems, in producing the series, employed a group of ten well known screenwriters, not one of whom ever violated the injunction against the use of the material for their own purposes.

In working on his Memoirs, Truman was on familiar ground with the printed word. In that medium he was comfortable and at home. But, in his TV experience, that was something else again for HST, and it baffled him. He said, "Perhaps we may have to forget the whole thing, but I would certainly hope not."

At this point, we were at a loss to find some way to arrange for the filming of the narrations by President Truman on TV. If HST had possessed the means, he would have done it on his own. Amidst this uncertainty, we received word that Bill Hillman had suffered a heart seizure and that his condition was critical. In a matter of days, on May 30, 1962, he died. This was a tragic loss to the President, his staff, and especially to me, as we had worked side by side through many years in a highly stimulating and privileged association with President Truman. It was HST's preference that there be no replacements for Hillman, for in his personal life he did not take too readily to new associates.

The prospects for producing the Truman Series had reached a low ebb. At the President's time of life, pursuing the project under these conditions would call for a drain on Truman's depleting energies that might pose a threat to his health. Just as we had decided to abandon our efforts, a special friend of Truman's, Abraham Feinberg, took it upon himself to persuade Screen Gems Television (where he had personal connections) to produce the series.

Feinberg's friendship with HST dated back to an event in 1948. Truman had been deeply involved in the process of according U.S. recognition to the evolving State of Israel, and was being beset by a stream of self-appointed spokesmen for the American Jewish community—an experience which the President found troublesome and distracting. He directed Matt Connelly, his Appointment Secretary, to close the calendar to all such petitioners. In spite of this injunction, Feinberg, a respected leader in the New York Jewish community, somehow managed to secure a visit with the President.

At the appointed hour, a tall, impressive man appeared at Matt Connelly's desk. "My name is Abraham Feinberg, and I'm pleased to meet you." This brought a smile to Connelly's face, and he asked him to have a seat. But, Feinberg, in the most ingenuous way, chose to walk around and greet everyone in the reception room—Secret Service men, guards, staff members, and even the White House historian and his secretary working quietly in an alcove (whom no one ever disturbed). To each he extended his hand and proclaimed, "My name is Abe Feinberg, and I'm pleased to meet you." Needless to say, this offbeat salutation brought a note of warmth and charm to this otherwise austere environment.

To the President, Feinberg was an unwelcome guest as he was shown into the Oval Office. Truman received him coolly with a stern, "What is it you want?"

Feinberg replied, "I just came to thank you, Mr. President, for everything you have already done." This unexpected expression of approval caught the President by surprise. He smiled and invited Feinberg to sit down. They had a long discussion which ranged over the many areas that touched on the Israeli problem.

The two got along so well that as Truman saw Feinberg out of his office, he stopped with him at Connelly's desk and said, "Matt, from now on, all matters that have to do with problems that relate to Israel should be cleared with Abraham Feinberg, and he will know what to do." A close relationship continued throughout the post presidential years, and it was a curious act of fate that fifteen years later, Feinberg was instrumental in reviving the prospects for the production of the series.

Then, in early 1963, I received a call at my home in Los Angeles from a Mr. Burt Schneider of Columbia Pictures, suggesting that he would like to explore with me the possibilities of underwriting the production of the Truman TV episodes. He and Robert Seidelman, who was in charge of sales for Screen Gems, came to my house the next evening and told me that they had carefully considered the prospect for such a series, and hoped to submit a proposal to President Truman if he was still interested in having the series produced.

I telephoned Truman the next day and told him about the development. Several days later, I again met with Schneider and Seidelman. They said that they realized there was little likelihood of interesting the networks in either producing or exhibiting this series, and that they concluded that syndication was the only way to attain wide distribution of the film. Syndication, they said, was a laborious process and an expensive one which called for a stringent production budget.

Screen Gems brought in Ben Gradus, a talented and experienced director/producer who proved to be an inspired choice. He quickly caught on to the thrust that HST hoped the series would take. There was a splendid personal adjustment from the start, and it was clear that Gradus was determined for Truman to have the fullest opportunity to express his own ideas in his own way.

At this point we were to suffer another tragedy. Our more recent associate and valued friend and communications expert, Charles L. Glett, was stricken (June 13, 1963) with a fatal malignancy. The loss of Hillman and Glett saddened HST. That was a dark and traumatic period for all of us.

It must have been an awesome ordeal for HST to sit through the filming and recording of all those 26 episodes. He did not do it from script; he did it strictly from memory. Yet he never flinched and never failed to appear at every one of the sessions. There were times when it was very difficult for him to perform; we could tell. Gradus was very attentive and very accommodating; yet he was always in control. It was hard to think of anyone else who could have been as skillful and knowledgeable as Gradus in achieving so much under such difficult and demanding circumstances.

The facilities were far from ideal; for reasons of economy most of the work was done in a basement studio in New York. Truman's submission to the ordeal was a measure of his conviction that the series needed to be produced in order to record the period as he lived it.

Of course, during the filming in New York, Truman attracted crowds wherever he went. When people saw him, at first they were incredulous, and many greeted him with the familiar "Hi, Harry!" Wherever he dined, restaurants would put up a sign: "Truman Ate Here." Sometimes on our walks to and from lunch, Bob Seidelman would accompany us. When the crowds began to bunch up, he would run interference proclaiming, "Yes, that's him; that's the President."

Truman never liked to be fussed over or embraced; a good handshake was all that was necessary. One day on his way back to the studio from lunch, he was stopped by a gentle, frail, old lady who said to him, "You aren't, are you?"

He answered, "I am what you think I am."

"Oh," she said, "could I please shake your hand?"

"Of course. I would be very pleased."

She wanted to shake hands with her bare hand, but there was a glove in the way which she tried to take off. It seemed to get stuck. He reassured her, "Now, take your time. There is no hurry." At last, the glove was off, and they shook hands.

But then the woman suddenly importuned, "Would you let me kiss you on the cheek, Mr. President?"

And he said, "If you like." And he stooped down so that she could reach his cheek. She was ecstatic as she walked off.

I turned to the President and said, "I would not have believed it if I had not seen it with my own eyes. You did something I never saw you do before."

His response was, "Did you see that woman's face? If I didn't let her, I would have hurt her and I couldn't do that."

Truman's naturalness and unpretentiousness won him the dedication of the production staff. During one of the filming sessions, a new man was engaged as audio engineer; he was a black man and kept totally to himself. In the course of the filming, I would occasionally step into his booth to ask him whether the President was coming through clearly. The response was always a curt yes or no.

At a break in the filming, when the group would gather around the President, this man would remain in his booth or off to one side. His reluctance to mingle with the group did not escape HST's attention. When the crew had broken for lunch, Truman beckoned the engineer to join him. When he came forward, HST said, "I've been wanting to meet you. Tell me something about yourself; where are you from?"

"You mean originally?" asked the man self-consciously.

Truman replied, "Originally we all came from the same source, but what part of the country do you hail from?" When he answered Kentucky, Truman picked it up immediately saying, "Oh, yes, some of my people came through Kentucky; some stayed there. I like that state." The man remained taciturn and ill at ease, but Truman continued, "Do you have any family here?"

The man said, "Yes, I have a twin brother."

Truman lighted up. "You know, I have a special interest in twins. Would it be possible for me to meet him, too? Could you bring him in with you tomorrow morning?"

The engineer was hesitant. "But, Mr. President, he is only a janitor!"

"Now, what in the world is wrong with being a janitor?" asked Truman. "It's an honorable occupation. It requires skill, and I'm sure that he's good at it. Please have him come, and there's no need for him to dress up. I would like to be photographed with both of you."

"I'll do my best, sir," said the engineer diffidently.

The next day when the two brothers came in to be photographed with Truman, they took up positions some distance from him. He asked them to come closer, but they only edged a bit nearer. HST reached out for their hands and pulled them towards him and signaled for the pictures to be taken.

The next morning when Truman got the prints, he called over the engineer and asked, "Would you autograph this picture to me and get your brother to sign it, too? I want to take it back home with me, and if you would like it, I will sign one for each of you."

Well, the transformation was electric. This man suddenly looked ten feet tall, and his reaction was all the more meaningful because he sensed that President Truman meant it.

After many months of filming, the completion was now in sight. It was becoming more and more evident that the project was exacting a terrible toll on HST's waning strength. However, the final result came through better than anyone had a right to expect, and much of the credit for that happy outcome was due, in large measure, to the dedication of the producer/director, Ben Gradus, and the superb skill of the film editor whose brilliant work earned him a special award from the Society of Film Editors.

Robert Seidelman performed a masterful job in managing the syndication of the series. He was able to achieve wide distribution in the United States, working at it city by city, and arranged a number of sales as well in many foreign countries. As Director of Sales for Screen Gems, he naturally did his best to recover the considerable investment involved. Yet it was clear to President Truman and to me that he was also motivated by the importance of the film to its potential viewers and to history. Some TV stations also viewed the series as an important public service. KDKA in Pittsburgh replaced a sponsored program with the noncommercial Truman Series.

With the TV series now in distribution, HST felt a sense of relief and a large measure of accomplishment from the knowledge that a personal account of the major events and decisions of his administration would be available to future generations in graphic form.

Having completed the filming of his 26 TV episodes, HST began to curtail his office hours and public appearances. To those of us who were close to him, it was evident that HST had begun to decline. Even during the filming of the episodes, especially as we neared the end, there were moments when he was showing signs of tiring and, on several occasions, of faltering. Nevertheless, he continued to tour the country on behalf of Democratic candidates. In that role, he worked hard, long hours and tirelessly, but it was evident that he was drawing on his reserves.

Eleanor Roosevelt

Mrs. Eleanor Roosevelt came to attend the wedding of her daughter Anna to Dr. James Halsted. It was a small private affair at a hideaway ranch in the Santa Monica mountains. After the ceremony, Mrs. Roosevelt, who was enjoying a morsel of wedding cake, turned to me and said, "Will you please convey to President Truman my warmest regards?" Then there was a pause, and she took on a very serious look. "There is something else I would like for you to tell President Truman for me."

I interposed, "You have no need for an intermediary between President Truman and yourself. I know of his high regard and esteem for you, for as you know, he has proclaimed you the 'First Lady of the World.'"

She replied, "I am rather hesitant about telling it to him myself, and I would like you to do it for me. Please tell him that in my judgment, he made a great President, and that I had earned the right to that assessment." Then there was a momentary reflection, "He faced up to some important issues that my own husband found it necessary to back away from."

With such a statement coming from Mrs. Roosevelt I felt it necessary to relay it to Mr. Truman immediately and for the moment he was genuinely pleased and overwhelmed.

As HST passed his eighty-fifth birthday, the time had come for him to forego his daily routine schedule and to go into seclusion. While there were no more office hours, his long time personal secretary, Rose Conway, made regular visits to the house and brought with her those matters that required his attention. From this time on, he was under the devoted care of his lifelong partner, Bess.

With Truman's passing, the world lost one of its great benefactors. In accordance with his wishes, he was laid to rest in the garden of the Truman Library in Independence. And, it was also his wish that he be given a simple burial, that there be no parades and no displays of any kind, and moreover, he was not to be taken to Washington for any ceremonial display. He died as he lived, an uncommon common man, who never lost touch with the common people.

ABOUT THE AUTHORS

David M. Noyes was born in 1898 and lived and was educated in and around Chicago. He was a newspaper and advertising executive, having owned small weeklies in the area and also worked for Foote Cone and Belding Advertising Agency. One of his clients was Senator Arthur Capper of the Capper Publications in Kansas.

He was called to Washington during the Roosevelt Administration to work with Donald M. Nelson on the War Production Board. It was on this job that he met and worked with Senator Harry Truman, Chairman of the Truman Commission, investigating Defense Agencies.

On FDR's death on April 12th, 1945, Noyes was called to the White House to attend the swearing in of Mr. Truman. He remained as an advisor and friend to Mr. Truman until his death. He was, along with others in the White House, an advisor on the Atom bomb, the Marshall Plan, creation of the CIA, firing of Douglas MacArthur, recognition of Israel, and the Potsdam Conference. (Contemporary Authors, Vol. 104).

Noyes was an advisor, biographer, and friend to Mr. Truman for 30 years. He was appointed counselor to Mr. Truman at the swearing in and remained at the White House in that capacity until 1953.

In the late 1960's he served Mr. Truman as advisor to the Peace Institute on Mt. Scopus. He helped Mr. Truman with his memoirs published in two volumes in 1955 and 1956 and another book, *Mr. Citizen*, in 1953. In 1946 Noyes produced a TV series entitled "Conflict, the Decisions of Harry Truman." Mr. Truman received the Eddie Award from the American Cinema Editors Society as the Outstanding Television Personality of the year. Mr. Noyes died in 1981 at his home in Los Angeles.

Edward J. Flynn is a California marketing and communications executive who worked with David Noyes over many years. He assisted Mr. Noyes in the writing and editing of these memoirs and finalized the writing after his death.

Flynn knew Mr. Truman from his initial Senatorial campaign in Columbia, Missouri, in 1934 for he was a student at the University of Missouri Journalism School.

As a consultant he represented the Standard oil Company, Motorola, UpJohn, and many other companies and was the Western Director of CARE.

He worked in Washington for several years on the campaigns of Mr. Truman, Kennedy, Johnson, and for GATT and NAFTA.

He is a keen political observer and has appeared on many radio, TV, cable, and talk shows and is currently on a lecture tour throughout the country.

He founded the Educational Broadcasting Station KCET Channel 28 in Los Angeles, and was one of the organizers of The Corporation for Public Broadcasting and the Advertising Council. He was one of the owners of radio station KRLA in Pasadena, California.

Lightning Source UK Ltd.
Milton Keynes UK
UKOW03f0811060614

232985UK00001B/43/A

9 780759 643819